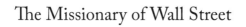

The Missionary of Wall Street

STEPHEN F. AUTH

THE
MISSIONARY
OF
WALL STREET

From Managing Money to Saving Souls
on the Streets of New York

SOPHIA INSTITUTE PRESS
Manchester, New Hampshire

Sophia Institute Press
Box 5284, Manchester, NH 03108
1-800-888-9344

www.SophiaInstitute.com

Sophia Institute Press® is a registered trademark of Sophia Institute.

Library of Congress Cataloging-in-Publication Data
To come.

First printing

For the souls we've encountered on the streets,
for my fellow missionaries,
and for Bob and Evelyn, without whom
neither the mission nor this book
would have been possible

Love never fails.

—1 Corinthians 13:8

Contents

The Missionary of Wall Street

The people and events described in the pages that follow are very real. With the exception of the missionaries themselves, however, all names, and sometimes descriptions, have been changed to protect their privacy.

1

No Longer Alone

Church of the Most Precious Blood, Baxter Alley,
Border of Little Italy and Chinatown, New York City
—December 2015, Monday night

Warm.
Dark.
Misty rain.
Fog.

A lone missionary heads up Baxter Street, past the front of the church, and stands quietly in the mist.

No one else is around.

About 6:45, a man dressed in dark clothes, bulging a bit in unnatural places, passes by, alone and in a hurry.

"Are you Catholic?" the missionary asks.

No reply.

He's Catholic.

The missionary pursues him. "Excuse me. Are you Catholic?"

"What?"

"Are you Catholic?"

"Yes. Sort of."

"Would you like to come into the church to pray? We have a beautiful manger scene in there."

"No. I can't do that. I have something on me that I can't take into a church. It would disrespect Him."

What a lead-in!

A conversation ensues.

Sox is an ex-con. Fifteen years in the slammer. An ex-con with a conscience well formed enough to know how to respect the Lord.

"Sox, one question. What happens if you get hit by a truck tonight?"

"If I get hit by a truck, I know He loves me and I'm going to Heaven."

"Sox, you have a very well-formed conscience. And you're bright besides. So work with me here. Right now you're doing something so bad that it would be disrespectful to enter the church."

"Right. I know what's right and wrong."

"And you're going to keep doing it."

"For now."

"And even though it would be disrespectful to enter the church, you think you can enter Heaven in this state?"

A long pause. "Uh ..."

"Sox? Sox, are you with me?"

Beads of sweat are appearing on Sox's brow.

"Look," he says at last. "I'm on a journey. I know I'm not where I need to be, but maybe I'll get there. I'm 20 percent better than I was ten years ago."

"Sox, that's good. That's real good. I'm also on a spiritual journey. And we're not alone. He's with us."

The missionary gives Sox a rosary to pray with — "Because," he tells him, "Mary is also with you, praying for you."

Sox knows how to pray the Rosary, but he asks if they can go through one decade for practice. He promises to pray the Rosary for Mary's protection. The missionary promises to pray every day for Sox, for his safe journey home.

"Now I have a question for you," Sox says. "Where did you come from? I went right by the church, I'm sure of it. Then suddenly you appeared out of the haze. Like an angel.... Are you an angel?"

"Sox, I was here, just as the Lord is here. He's always here. He's waiting for you. You just have to open the door."

And with that, Sox, a rosary in his hand and a prayer in His heart, walks off into the warm, damp darkness of Baxter Street In a hurry.

But no longer alone.

∞

What did Sox end up doing that night?

And where is he today?

I don't know.

And what was I, a senior executive with one of the country's largest money managers, armed with nothing more than a handful of rosaries, doing hailing an ex-con packing heat in a dark alley near Chinatown on a warm December night?

I don't know the answer to that one either.

I'm still trying to figure it out.

∞

*Saint Barnabas Hospital, Livingston, New Jersey
—Thanksgiving 2002*

The day my heart nearly stopped.

I had been closing in on the end of another very busy year at work. I had recently taken on the job of chief investment officer of equities, replacing two predecessors who had split the work between them. The bear market that had begun two years before was still grinding to new lows, and too many of our portfolios were performing badly. Staffing changes loomed.

At the same time, my two young sons, Richard and Michael, were fast becoming young men. They needed fathering. But with portfolio managers spread between Pittsburgh and New York, I found myself in the air almost as often as I was on the ground.

A strong faith might have me helped me at this point, and I wish I could tell you that I had one.

I didn't.

After falling into an indifferent agnosticism through my four years at Princeton, I had come back to the Church enough to get married in it to the girl of my dreams, Evelyn. She was a devout Catholic.

As for me, I did my best to get to Sunday Mass regularly— when it was convenient. But I kept God in my Sunday-morning box. The other six and a half days of the week were mine.

In short, I had no deep love of Jesus in my heart.

I suppose you could say I didn't have a heart.

∽

All this changed in November 2002, when my heart literally stopped. Electrical malfunction. That meant twelve days in the cardiac care unit at St. Barnabas Hospital, the first several of which were spent on my back, hooked up to a variety of electrodes designed to keep me alive, while a bevy of interns read the monitors over my head with increasing terror and relayed the data back to my cardiologist, who was at home for the Thanksgiving holiday.

The doctors at St. Barnabas are quite good, and eventually they determined that I suffered from a relatively rare but potentially fatal, heart arrhythmia. Once they figured that out, they fixed me.

On Thanksgiving Day, during this crisis, a priest visited me in the hospital. I had met him only recently at an affair in New York City, but he drove five hours from his mother's house in Maryland to visit me and give me sacramental anointing of the sick. That meeting changed my life.

I had been way too busy for God. Now, with a potential near-term encounter with the Eternal looming, receiving the anointing of the sick seemed like a good idea. Of course, this also entailed the sacrament of confession, which I hadn't received in many years.

I don't remember what sins I confessed to Fr. John Connor that afternoon, but they were probably very general, and there probably weren't very many of them. When you've been away from God for a long time, you begin to trust yourself and your judgment so much that you gradually lose track of which behaviors and habits are OK to you that might not be OK to Him.

But I did my best to give a good confession, and Fr. John was very gentle with me. After I had received the sacraments, we had a long chat.

"Steve," he said, "this is a wake-up call from God. Take it as such. You were meant to do more for Him, to give more to Him. You're wasting your talents. You're being very selfish with the gifts He's given you."

Lying there in that hospital bed, not knowing where the next few days would take me, I had plenty of time to ponder Father's words. I knew I had to do something different with my life. I really didn't know what it would be, but I did know it would lead to places I didn't want to go. I knew it would take me out of my comfortable Steve-centered world.

I was afraid of that.

What would I have to give up?

What sacrifices would I have to make?

I knew I'd have to make them.

"The Lord is calling," I thought to myself. "I don't know where He wants to lead me. But I will go."

2

Be Not Afraid

Pittsburgh. The Duquesne Club
—March 2009

I had spent a long day dealing with yet another aftershock of the great financial collapse of 2008–2009. Now I was ready to collapse in my room in the city's most luxurious club. I had had enough stress and worry for the day. I called Evelyn to check in.

She sounded excited. "I signed us up to do a mission in New York!" she exclaimed.

"What?"

"A Holy Week mission—you know, like the ones you did down in Mexico. I figured you knew how to do missions, so I said yes when Father called and said he needed help."

She made it sound so simple. And it was true that I had been doing missions in Mexico. After my near-death experience, I had tried to take my wake-up call seriously. The rest of my family had been involved with the Regnum Christi movement,[1] and when

---

[1] Regnum Christi is an ecclesial movement, made up of nearly twenty-five thousand members worldwide, consisting of four vocations: Legionaries of Christ, consecrated women, consecrated men, and lay members. In this text, we often refer to the lay members as Regnum Christi "adults" or "teams" or "teens."

my then-teenage son Michael went on a mission to Mexico, I went too.

But this was different.

"Sweetheart — dear — are you out of your mind? What are we going to do — stand on street corners and look for Catholics?"

"Well … yes."

"Sweetie, do you have any idea what you're talking about? New York is *nothing* like Mexico. In Mexico, we're just trying to be sure we get to every house of our assigned village so that no one's feelings get hurt. *Everyone* in Mexico is Catholic. They're inviting us into their homes. They're feeding us. *They're* the ones ministering to *us*!

"But New York — I know New York. There's no way in the world this could *ever* work. No one in New York cares about stuff like this. We'll be standing on a street corner having cigars put out on our foreheads the whole hour."

"It's not an hour. It's for the whole Triduum — Holy Thursday, Good Friday, and Holy Saturday."

"What?" I must have been shouting into the phone. "Have you gone mad? Call him back and tell him no. Better yet, tell him *absolutely* no. No way, no how. Not going. I am *not* going to do this."

∞

SoHo, New York
— Good Friday 2009

Here I was with Evelyn ready to go out into the streets for our Holy Week mission. And I was still trying to figure out what we were doing here.

When I realized there was no hope of convincing Ev that we weren't going, I quickly called my good friend Bob Infanger and told him he needed to come too. Bob works on a big trading desk at a major Wall Street firm, and believe me, in the spring of 2009—when we were still reeling from the biggest financial crisis since the Great Depression—he had other things to do. But Bob had been with me on the Mexico missions, where we had developed a close bond. If I was the realist, Bob was the eternal optimist.

Bob came.

What were we doing?

The mission had no lay leadership. The man behind it was the endearing and charismatic Msgr. Donald Sakano, the energetic new pastor of Old St. Patrick's on Mulberry Street, who saw that his new parish was struggling to be relevant in a neighborhood that was becoming rapidly secularized. He had a vision of what needed to be done—but not necessarily a plan.

In fact, the closest thing he had to a plan was to send as many Regnum Christi adults and teens as possible out into the streets of SoHo, while the priests—Msgr. Sakano and three others—manned the confessionals.

The rest was up to the Holy Spirit.

We didn't get much done that Holy Thursday.

By the time we got semiorganized and out on the street, it was time to get to the Mass of the Lord's Supper. So, all we accomplished was alerting the neighborhood that some Jesus people in mission shirts and jeans were in the area.

∞

So today—Good Friday—is our first real day on the street. And it gets off to a dark start.

A few of us try to set up a promotion station on the corner of Prince and Mott, against the walls of Old St. Patrick's. We consider this home turf, since we are passing out pamphlets with the Triduum service schedule.

The vendor with the hat stand on the same corner has other ideas. He points out that he has paid the city for the right to hawk his hats, and he says our presence is going to drive away potential customers.

"Go across the street!" he barks.

We meekly do.

Later, I am standing on Prince at the entrance to the parish school—again, home turf, but this doesn't prove any easier. A thin, middle-aged woman with an angry look on her face, and not a believer, glares at me as I offer her a rosary and as she passes yells, "What are you doing about that pope of yours? You Catholics are all a bunch of pedophiles!"

Yes, this is working out roughly as I had predicted.

Yet, as the day wears on, parts of the neighborhood seem to warm to us. The arrival of our teens certainly makes a difference. Father Richard, one of the priests running the mission, sends me and the teens out to SoHo to "find an abortion clinic." We don't, but we station ourselves near a busy subway stop instead, and there we at least get a few smiles and words of encouragement.

Still, out here among the busy holiday shoppers (most of whom seem to have no idea what the holiday is about), "not interested" is the most common reaction.

For a break, I head back to the church, where I find many of our missionaries huddled behind its protective walls.

I take shelter there too.

The original St. Patrick's Cathedral—known more formally as the Basilica of St. Patrick's Old Cathedral—was built in the early 1800s, mostly with thousands of small donations from local Irish and Italian immigrants. It's surrounded by a fortress-like, ten-foot-high brick wall, which once was used for defense. Earlier generations of English and Dutch Protestants saw Irish Catholic immigrants coming into their neighborhood as a threat to their American way of life. Anti-Catholic riots were common.

Now we don't have to worry about riots. But over the years, as the neighborhood grew increasingly secular, the parish seemed to retreat inside that wall surrounding the church.

It's safe there.

It's comfortable.

We can deal with it.

But Christ called us to proclaim that "the kingdom of heaven is at hand" (Matt. 3:2). That was what our mission was about.

So we had a choice to make.

We could stay in our comfort zone, in our holy huddle, as the world around us slipped into a secularism that aims to eradicate God completely. We could build a wall around us, even higher than the one around Old St. Pat's, and try to stay holy within it.

That approach might get us to Heaven — but it certainly wouldn't bring many more with us.

The other choice was to lock arms as brothers and sisters in Christ, advance with determination outside the wall, and let God work through us to grow the Kingdom.

It's messy outside the wall.

It's mixed up.

It's tough-going.

It's full of people who are walking alone, indifferent at best, often hostile.

But that's where Christ is.

Outside the wall.

Out there on the streets.

∞

Perseverance is the greatest challenge for most new missionaries. We're not used to cold-calling strangers out in the street. We're most likely not used to being so blatantly ignored, stared down, called fools, or worse.

So, many of the most well-intentioned first-timers begin seeking shelter after the first thirty minutes.

"Time for a coffee break!" "Is anyone hungry?" "Let's try another corner."

The harsh reality is that, for every successful encounter on the streets of SoHo, our missionaries are rejected or ignored or yelled at by a minimum of twenty passersby, an average of forty, and on some nights eighty or a hundred. We're not used to that kind of treatment.

On top of our natural human reactions to that abuse in the streets, add the role of the devil. Rest assured, the devil is not happy about our new evangelization. Most of the souls we encounter are on some level of his slippery slope — some are near the bottom, convinced they're lost, or even no longer aware of eternity and their impending lost future. Others are near the top of the slope, only recently beginning some sinful habit that seems innocent enough right now. Most are practicing a reasonably sophisticated form of rationalization, convincing themselves that, for some reason or another, their behavior is morally acceptable.

The devil is actively engaged with them in this dialogue.

The last thing the devil wants is some pesky missionary, fueled by the Holy Spirit, disrupting his prey and shocking them into a return to grace. When the devil sees a new missionary arrive, that missionary has a large target on his back. From that minute on, the devil works hard to get that missionary off the streets.

His most effective weapon is fear.

On the back of our mission T-shirts, emblazoned in big letters under an image of Christ on the Cross, are three words: BE NOT AFRAID.

For sure, there are occasionally good reasons to be fearful on the streets of New York. When I spent that lonely night in the fog in 2015—the night I met Sox—I admit I feared for my safety.

More often, fear of embarrassment plagues us.

Fear of being ignored.

Fear of being insulted.

Fear of our egos' being shamed.

Fear of being recognized.

All these fears—and then some—are ones that those of us on the mission have felt at one time or another.

Fear works against our effectiveness as missionaries. People passing by can sense it, almost smell it. Like sharks circling a wounded fish, they may even delight in exploiting it. A passerby who might have been interested in confession—but was a little afraid himself—may sense a missionary's fear and back off. With a tendency to speak in hardly audible tones and to withdraw from the crowd, a fearful missionary can barely get anyone's attention. As the night wears on, that initial fear is reinforced by the occasional bite from a passing shark, and the missionary withdraws more.

All this is obvious. But how can we escape the fear trap?

The answer—as with most aspects of the Christian life—lies in the heart of Jesus.

Jesus faced all these fears, and a thousand times worse, on the long walk to Calvary. He has been there. He knows what we're going through. So the answer to fear is to connect with Jesus. Lean on Him. Know and believe that He is with you, protecting you. Embrace your fear, and then give it to Christ. He will free you to "be not afraid." Confident in His grace, you can then confidently extend that grace to others.

For several years now, we've organized our mission around the protective wall of Old St. Pat's. This imposing brick structure presents a useful image of how a faith community protects itself. Indeed, many of us Catholics—or, more broadly, many people of faith—have our own personally protective walls: our parish prayer groups or, if we are members of a Church movement such as Regnum Christi or Opus Dei, our small encounter teams. These rich support networks give us welcome succor in our battles to remain faithful in a world without faith. That's a big help, but we can't stay inside. We must go out into the streets, and we must keep going even when everything else seems to be trying to drive us back inside.

Early in my missionary work, my first instinct was to practice what I call the "white knuckle method" of perseverance. Tough it out, grit through it, fight back.

Sometimes the devil would win, and I'd take a break.

More often than not, I'd manage to white-knuckle my way through the evening long enough to find a potential penitent. The problem was that, by then, I was so stressed out and in such a bad mood that I was unable to get that person into the church.

So now I use what I call the "Holy Spirit approach." Before we head to the streets, I stop in the church to pray, maybe even go to confession. I put myself in the hands of the Holy Spirit and ask Him to carry me through. When I do this sincerely and with deep faith, I always find I have joyful, confident perseverance through the long night of darkness.

Once you have the habit of joyful perseverance, you'll keep going even when everything seems to be working against you. Even the weather.

Then success will sneak up on you and surprise you.

Be Not Afraid

∞

St. Patrick's Old Cathedral, SoHo
—Advent, 2013

It was a white Christmas in SoHo. The cold snow started blowing midmorning, and just kept blowing as the day advanced. There were nearly twenty of us on the streets, along with four priests in the confessionals, but we weren't having much success. The snow not only made holding our posts a physical challenge. It also kept the passersby moving and hard to engage. Our capture rate dropped from one-in-twenty to one-in-forty; suddenly, hardly anyone was Catholic.

And then, success.

One of our new young people asked, "Are you a Catholic?" and the answer was yes.

She turned to her brother.

"I found a Catholic!" she told him excitedly. "What do I do now?"

3

Loving and Thinking

How We Organize a Mission

What do I do now?

Our first New York City mission was largely chaos. None of us knew what to do. We had no plan, no script. As I had anticipated, the crowd was rough on us.

It seemed to me that we had accomplished little more than to stir things up. Msgr. Sakano, on the other hand, was inspired. Catholics out on the streets, evangelizing! This itself was a statement. And we were getting encouraging reports from parishioners. Despite the chaos, we had accomplished something.

So, rather than grow discouraged, we dug in and resolved to do better next time. But as we kept going out, year after year, we started to understand what worked. The common element was love.

Fearless perseverance keeps us at our post and gives us the chance to engage in an encounter with a lost soul on the street. Love draws that soul in.

In today's world of *me first*, love — true love — is in short supply. Lost souls hunger for love. And when they sense true love in the spirit of a missionary on the street, inevitably they're drawn in.

THE MISSIONARY OF WALL STREET

How can we develop this attitude of love? Again—no surprise—we come back to the heart of Jesus. Jesus' deep, self-giving, *agape* for us in that great big heart of His is the love we must give to others. We need to find that love in us, and on the street it needs to flow out of us, genuinely. We need to see Christ's loving face in the face of every passerby on the street—the ones who stop to talk with us, but also the ones who ignore us, hurry past us, or even insult us.

Of all the elements in the heart of a missionary, love of others is what most distinguishes us from the crowd. By itself, this often turns the tide. When a casual passerby feels that love, it prompts a stirring deep inside the person's soul, an impulse to stop and talk to us. All of us want to be loved, and most of us are not loved enough. So, when someone feels love in the air, he stops to enjoy it, to embrace it. That's the beginning of an incredible encounter in the streets.

That's why, if I have time to give a missionary only one instruction, I always say, "Love, don't think."

But we're even more effective if someone coordinating the group has done some thinking beforehand.

∞

Saint Patrick's Old Cathedral, SoHo
—Holy Wednesday 2015

Today the pope arrived.

Our little band out on Prince and Mott was reinforced from all sides: men from the New York chapter of the Lumen Institute,[2]

---

[2] The Lumen Institute provides faith-based formation for business leaders across the United States.

men's and women's teams from Regnum Christi in New Jersey, the St. Patrick's (Chatham) Men's Gospel group, and the *coup de grace*—all forty joyous, Christ-filled brothers from the Cheshire, Connecticut, seminary.

For extra insurance, the brothers brought the pope.

Not exactly the pope, but a life-size, super-high-resolution cardboard cutout that turned the neighborhood upside down. Out on Lafayette and Prince, usually one of our toughest stations, the brothers were having a joyous time with the hundreds of passersby, many of whom were taking selfies with Pope Francis while the rest of the team evangelized. Later that night, I showed some of the photos to the missionary in the back of the church, and she recognized in one of the pictures someone who had visited the church later in the night, a young man who told her he is a Sunni Muslim. The pope appeals to all.

By the time the Regnum Christi teams arrived, the neighborhood was hopping. I almost felt sorry for the unbelievers and the atheists. They were outmanned. And some of them were already posting their pope selfies on Facebook.

So we found a good opening. That's important. The first challenge out there on the streets is simply to entice someone to stop and talk while he's hurrying by in his own little world.

We always make sure that we wear the mission uniform, which, in our case, is jeans and sneakers with a Regnum Christi mission shirt emblazoned at the back with an image of Christ on the Cross and the words "Be Not Afraid." The uniform instantly helps us stand out in the crowd and signals to a passerby that this is not likely to be a casual encounter with a random street hawker.

Generally, we missionaries go out in twos or threes, back to back, to cover pedestrian traffic in all directions on our corner.

Body language as someone approaches is important. We try to stand in a relaxed posture, with a smile on our faces. If we are tensed up as if awaiting an appointment with the guillotine's blade, we are more likely to have one land on our neck.

As soon as the soul we're targeting gets within earshot, we try to lock eyes lovingly and use our "pickup line." We have a variety of lines, depending on the situation and what makes us comfortable. The most efficient line, and the one we use most often, is simply "Are you Catholic?" Although occasionally non-Catholics take offense at this question, it has the ready benefit of quickly sorting the crowd and focusing our attention.

We find that most Catholics, when asked, will admit they are Catholic, or at least that they were Catholic. We even find that the Catholics who deny that they are Catholic often feel guilty about doing so within a few blocks and come back to the corner to admit they are. Even with offended non-Catholics, we've been able to use their initial hostility to open a conversation, which often leads at least to a church visit.

Another pickup line is "Would you like a rosary?" We keep our rosaries fully displayed on our arms, and often passersby approach us for one, thus initiating a conversation. Some missionaries start with this rosary question; others use it as a second question once someone has expressed interest in a brief chat.

We also sometimes ask passersby if they would like a schedule of services for Holy Week (or Advent, or San Gennaro, or whatever is appropriate). This is a little less intimidating, but it usually ends in a quick handoff of the pamphlet, and no deeper dialogue develops.

Our priests offer Adoration of the Blessed Sacrament most of the evenings when we are evangelizing, and for it we offer church visitors votive candles to place in front of the altar in a cross pattern while they say a prayer. For most Catholics and ex-Catholics, lighting a candle in church is one of their most comforting memories, so we generally get positive responses when we offer votive prayer candles. People even love to help when we ask them nicely. We've had great success in getting people to church just by saying, "We're trying to make a cross of prayer candles in the church here. Can you help? It'll just take a minute!"

Farther from the church, in the byways of the parish, we use all of the above, along with a few other props to carry the church out into the neighborhood. We have a cross, which we either carry about the neighborhood or hold prominently on a street corner. Others on the "cross team" will carry a basket and a pad of paper, so we can offer people the chance to write a prayer, and pin or tape it to the cross. We use this especially on Good Friday in the cross walk from midtown, and we do a morning cross walk in the parish on Holy Saturday. On other nights, we just send out a team to stay with the cross on a particularly busy street corner. People generally respond well to a request for a prayer intention, even when they would otherwise have no interest in going to church themselves. After all, who does not have a prayer in his heart?

Then, of course, there's the pope.

I was initially suspicious of the idea of a life-sized pope cutout. It was introduced by a team of seminarians who brought the pope with them one "Spy Wednesday" night. But the evening was a huge success, and I had to admit I was wrong. We also collect prayer intentions at the station where we set up the pope.

Jesus often used the fishing metaphor when describing His mission, and so do we, His missionaries. There are certainly many paths to hooking a fish, some gentle, some direct, some fast, some slow, some stern, some with laughter. Over time you'll develop a method that's comfortable, and even better, you'll learn to adjust your method to the person you're trying to hook. More on this in the pages to come.

Just remember that you must persevere. Don't get discouraged by the first rejection, or the thirtieth. Our experience in SoHo is that, on any given night, it can take twenty to forty passersby to get one positive response to any of our approaches. In your city or neighborhood the response rate could be more or less—but it will never be anything like what you're hoping for.

Whatever pickup line you use, never deliver it with impatience, anger, frustration, or fear in your heart. That will not work. The trick to hooking a fish lies in putting the last rejection behind you quickly: reset your hook and move on lovingly and joyfully to the next approaching soul. "Shake the dust from your feet" (Matt. 10:14) and move on. If you persevere with your missionary heart fully engaged, the next big fish could be about to hit your line.

These are strategies we use as individuals, but it helps a lot if someone has made an overall plan, so together we can be as effective as possible.

∞

After our initial confusion on the streets, we gradually adopted a staged plan for creating a "human net" to catch souls.

Our first step was to observe pedestrian patterns in the neighborhood. Where is the primary traffic? How many people move through the area?

Then we developed a street map of the parish and identified key intersections where missionaries were needed.

One thing we learned after a while was that our stations needed to be staged in such a way that we had complete but not duplicate coverage of passersby. What we found was that most pedestrians passing through the neighborhood would at least tolerate being hailed at some point by a missionary. But if we staged our missionaries in such a way that they were likely to be hailed multiple times within a short distance, they felt as if they were running the gauntlet, and we generated more ill will than conversations.

So, we learned to set up our missionary stations in a giant diagonal crisscross pattern. At any given intersection, we always stage our missionaries on diagonal corners so that pedestrians passing through the intersection engage a missionary once, not twice. On a larger scale, we stage the intersections diagonally as well, so that a pedestrian who makes it through one station and goes on in a straight line won't hit another missionary intersection for at least two blocks. This diagonal matrix extends out several blocks in ever-larger concentric circles, enveloping the parish.

Far off in those outer stations at the edge of the parish, it's more difficult to turn souls all the way to the church—although we certainly have missionaries who've managed to do it. Nevertheless, these stations tend to be critical to the power of the overall net. They ensure that all the pedestrians passing through the parish have encountered a missionary at least once. Perhaps they've been asked if they have a prayer intention. Possibly they've been invited to visit the church. Sometimes they may even have been asked if they'd like to receive the sacrament of reconciliation.

It often happens that, even when souls have politely passed by with a "not interested" or maybe even no word at all, the Holy Spirit has already entered their hearts, and they're thinking about the possibility. Later, if the net is formed properly, they'll run into a second team, and they're often more open to talking by then.

At the center of this human net is always what we call the "hot corner," the one closest to the front door of the church. We find that, with the church this close, the Holy Spirit is particularly active. It's less of a struggle to get a soul to commit to a visit when he can see the front door just a short distance away. Missionaries on this corner don't just alert passersby to the services available: our aim is to seek commitments to receive reconciliation or at least to pray in the church. In some cases, we walk fearful or hesitant souls right into the church. Our goal is to get them into the Lord's house — preferably for confession, but even if it's only for a candle lighting, we've won a victory.

Inside the church are four final stations that don't seem like stations at all. At the head of the nave, near the altar and visible as soon as you enter the church, we station the prayer team. These are missionaries who are very connected to Jesus through prayer, but for different reasons may not desire or be able to work the streets. I always remind our missionaries that the patron saint of all missionaries is St. Thérèse of Lisieux, a cloistered nun. No mission of evangelization can succeed without prayer, and the prayer team's help is critical.

A second team is the Adoration candle team, also in the front, passing out candles to light in front of the Blessed Sacrament. Our Adoration team keeps a notepad and pencils and asks people to write intentions and leave them in a basket before the Blessed Sacrament. As people from the streets get their candles and kneel before the Blessed Sacrament, they become, in effect, part of the prayer team.

Our third team is placed in the back of the church, greeting people as they come in and ushering them to the Adoration team — or, if they are seeking reconciliation, to one of the priests. This team in the back is a pivotal link in the net. We often call them "the closers." We find that, once they're inside, even souls who came into the church only to light a candle and pray are often moved by the Holy Spirit to want more. They are too embarrassed to go directly to confession but will often do so gladly when invited gently. Sometimes they'll tell a missionary in the back of the church that they don't know how to begin, and in these cases, we kneel beside them and walk them through an examination of conscience to prepare them. We usually post only one missionary, or at most two, in the back of the church; if there are too many, prospective penitents feel more intimidated than supported.

Our final team, of course, is the priests themselves. Waiting patiently in the confessionals, *in persona Christi* (in the person of Christ), they lovingly hear the confessions—often twenty, thirty, forty, and even sixty years of sins—and dispense the Lord's mercy.

It goes without saying that this team is by far the most important. The key is to have holy priests who love to hear confessions and know how to give solid advice while displaying the Lord's mercy in a big way. With many of our penitents having been away from the sacrament for a long time, these priests need to be confession veterans who are not easily shocked. Many of the penitents we bring to confession have had a bad experience with the sacrament or are expecting to get hit over the head with a baseball bat because of some sin they've committed. That's why gentle priests are vital![3]

[3] In SoHo, the parish priests have often been reinforced by priests from the Legionaries of Christ, the priestly order of Regnum Christi.

The mission leader organizes this net. First, he must place the right people in the right spots.

Many first-timers to the mission are not yet comfortable with engaging in a deep dialogue about spiritual matters with perfect strangers on the streets. But they are joyful, confident in their faith, and ready to persevere. These are good candidates for the peripheral stations, which start the whole process rolling.

Missionaries in the center need to be both the most experienced and the most comfortable with engaging strangers in conversation. Fortunately, in New York, our ranks are full of businesspeople who do that for a living, and it's just a matter of helping them figure out how to employ this skill in a different context. Most figure it out quickly.

In the back of the church we station what I call the "gentle souls"—usually well-formed Regnum Christi members who have a soft touch and evoke the meekness of Christ. Their job is to encourage souls, gently and lovingly, to take the last, toughest step into the confessional. They are the center of the net. Find the gentle souls on your team and place them there.

Of the quarter-million or so people to whom we witness in a week's mission in SoHo, each has a unique temperament, a different past, and a special "problem." It is possible, even likely, that just one particular missionary has the right mix of background, skills, and personality to bring in any one of these lost souls.

Are you that missionary? In your neighborhood, there may be someone waiting for you, someone you're uniquely suited for.

Do you think you can do it?

Do you have what it takes to be a missionary?

4

Can I Really Be a Missionary?

Corner of Prince and Mott
—Holy Saturday 2013

Three ten- to twelve-year-olds show up at the missionary station on the corner. They had been at the church with their parents, but they say they want to be closer to the action.

So we start them hailing passersby, and they turn out to be better at it than we are. They cut to the chase right away.

"Excuse me, sir, are you Catholic?"

"No."

On to the next prospect without pausing. "Excuse me, ma'am, are you Catholic?"

"No."

The kids aren't discouraged. They just keep going. "Excuse me, are you Catholic?"

"Uh ... yes."

"Great! Would you like a rosary?"

"Oh, yes! Thank you!"

"Have you confessed?"

"What? Confession? Oh, I don't do that!"

But then they do.

We start to haul in two fish at a time.

And we find that these kids are so engaging and joyful that they're especially good at accompanying the nervous ones—still wriggling on the hook—on the "confession walk" to one of our missionaries at the back of the church. The children even help the passersby to prepare for the gift of Christ's forgiveness, telling them how to say the Act of Contrition.

If those children can do it, you can, too.

If you decide to take up the challenge of a street mission where you live, you must first seek the *missionary heart and attitude*. Heart and attitude are two sides of a coin. The heart is what is inside you, and the attitude is what others perceive as you approach them. When you've found your missionary heart, your missionary attitude will flow naturally from within.

Where is your missionary heart?

It's the heart of Jesus in us.

Each of us will find our heart in a different way, but here are ten elements that seem to be part of every successful missionary's story.

Willingness to Answer the Call

I can't tell you how many times I've said to myself, "I'm not holy enough for that job" or "That's not my gift" or "That's over my head." I'm sure the number is in the hundreds.

All of us receive a spiritual call at some point—a call such as the one I got back in 2009 when my wife told me she had volunteered us for a New York street mission. Most of us respond as I did: "Absolutely not. No way, no how. Not going."

But if there's one truth I've learned as a missionary of Christ, it's this: none of us are qualified for this job. Only Christ is. None of us can convert a lost soul. Only Christ can.

If that's true, then it's prideful to think we *can't* do this but can do something else in its place. We can do *anything* ... but only through Him.

The reality is that Christ is pinging us all the time. He was pinging me in that hospital bed in St. Barnabas. He was pinging me a little louder when Evelyn called me up at the Duquesne Club to ask me to join the mission in New York. I don't want to think about how many pings I haven't even recognized.

So, the first step to developing your missionary heart is to stop analyzing each ring of the phone. Don't ask whether you should pick it up. Don't ask whether you're qualified for the job. Get off your high horse and begin to understand that "the Lord does not call the equipped; he equips the called."

Pick up the phone.

Answer the call.

Prayer and Silence

Have you spent any time reading lives of the saints? If you have, you must have noticed a common denominator in their spiritual lives: considerable time spent in silent prayer. Jesus Himself is the ultimate guide for us here: He often began His great miracles with long periods of silent prayer and ended them the same way. Through the din of the hustle-and-bustle world around us, only in silent prayer can you truly hear His whispering voice.

My first silent retreat, just before that first SoHo mission, was a revelation for me. I'm used to talking and discussing all day, so at first I found the retreat uncomfortable. Gradually, in the silence of that little chapel, I heard God speaking to me—giving me my marching orders, if you will.

In retrospect, that special sense of connectedness served me well in the mission that followed. So, if you're planning to go on a street mission, do a lot of praying in advance. Get yourself as connected as possible to your Creator. Maybe even go on a silent retreat. You're trying to meld with His heart, and you need to give Him a chance to reach you.

Reception of the Sacrament of Reconciliation

This may seem obvious to you, but it wasn't to me: only by receiving the graces of the sacrament of reconciliation can you be effective in offering it to others. You can't give what you don't have.

Over the years, I've watched many missionaries in the streets.

Some seem incredibly effective; others less so. When I see missionaries who aren't doing so well, I often ask them quietly at some point, "Have you had a chance to get to confession yet yourself?" Invariably, the answer comes back: "No, not yet."

Right then and there, I gently push them into the church. More often than not, they return energized, joyful, and a lot more effective.

In my case, I had a chance at that silent retreat to participate for the first time in St. Ignatius Loyola's Spiritual Exercises. In those Exercises, the retreat master gives penitents the opportunity to offer a general confession — a confession or re-confession of all the sins of our past up to that point.

For me, that was huge. I had been lugging around a lot of baggage from times long past, but those sins are never forgotten, and they weighed me down. But here was the upside for me: the bigger the list of sins forgiven, the deeper the sense of mercy received; and the deeper that sense, the more powerful the desire to give others the chance to receive that mercy.

Maybe it's no coincidence that the first two Fathers of the Church, Peter and Paul, were such sinners in the beginning.

They must have felt an especially profound healing from Jesus. I suspect that their depth of gratitude and love energized their love for others.

Now, your spiritual life may be in good shape. You may need only a light wash before heading into the streets. Even so, go and receive the sacrament. Its message of mercy and love is a key element of the heart of every missionary.

And if you really want a rocket booster, try making a general confession instead. You may find yourself in an entirely different orbit.

Shared Experience with Jesus

All good relationships deepen and grow with two key elements: communication and shared experiences. In our relationship with God, prayer is the communication part. Mission is the shared experience.

Time and again, the most joyful missionaries I encounter, bubbling over with their street stories, tell me, "Steve, I felt Jesus' presence there with me!"

I certainly felt the Lord's presence alone in the dark on Baxter Street when I hailed an ex-con packing a gun. How else could I have been so completely relaxed and confident?

If you want to develop the heart of a missionary, be attentive to Jesus' presence. Jesus *is* there with you. Feel Him, smell Him, become Him. It's His heart you're after. And here's the bonus: the more often you answer the call and the more you come forth from your protective walls and enter the streets with Jesus at your side, the more shared experiences with Him you will have and the closer to Him you will become. In helping others to find a relationship with Christ, your relationship with Him will grow and deepen. His heart will become yours.

Willingness to Embrace Suffering

We don't like to suffer. We're programmed to avoid pain at nearly all costs. But we all suffer at some point. It's the human condition. So, while you certainly should do what you can to alleviate your suffering, you should also embrace it.

I've always heard Christ speak to me most clearly when I was suffering—such as when I was in the hospital dealing with heart failure. And, of course, there can be plenty of suffering in the mission itself—all that putting cigars out on our foreheads that I worried so much about.

I'm not sure why it is that we hear Jesus most clearly when we're suffering, but it could be that in suffering we get a little closer to the heart of Jesus on the Cross. We feel His pain—in a small, small way, to be sure—but we feel it nonetheless.

So, if you want to develop your missionary heart, the next time you're suffering, embrace it.

Pray to Him.

And thank Him for letting you share His pain.

Love

I've already devoted a chapter to love. A few more words here: the secret to the heart of a missionary is love. You must love everyone you see. No exceptions.

How do you do that? How can you possibly love *everyone*, especially the rude and disrespectful ones who stream past you in SoHo thinking you're some homeless person from the Bowery?

The only answer I have is the heart of Jesus that is within each of us.

Find His heart in yourself. Then let it pour out on the streets, instinctively, from within you. "Love, don't think."

There is literally no argument more eloquent, more persuasive, for bringing in a lost sheep. The people we meet on the streets often have a lot of material possessions, but far too many of them feel unloved. As your encounter deepens, as you probe someone with heartfelt questions, most people respond from their hearts. They begin to ask themselves, "What is the guy doing here? He's enduring weather, hunger, scorn—for me?" Inevitably, the love of the missionary begets love from the passerby. And a casual meeting on a street corner is transformed into something much more profound.

Joy

We Catholics suffer from a serious branding problem. Ask someone to describe what a Catholic is like, and the first response you get might be "guilt-ridden." "They're always dragging themselves through the mud," people might say. "They deny themselves all the fun things in life."

Pope Francis is on to this, and it's probably the reason why his very first papal letter was entitled *The Joy of the Gospel*. Committed Catholics know that, far from making them miserable, their Faith makes them joyful. Connected with Jesus and following His Way, they're becoming the perfect, happy souls that God, their Creator, made them to be. They're finding their true selves, and there is great joy in that.

This is the Joy of the Gospel, and it's the message the pope wants us to project in our evangelization efforts. So many times on the streets of New York, I've heard people say, "Wow! This is amazing! We didn't know Catholics did this sort of thing! You guys look so happy!" There's nothing more compelling to the beaten-down souls wandering the streets of New York than joy.

Sometimes I tell our young people when they wonder what to say out there, "Don't say anything. Just be your joyful selves.

People will come up to you and start a conversation." Incredibly, this works. People see a joyful missionary and a voice inside them says, "Go to her. Get me some of that!"

Perseverance

We discussed one angle on perseverance in chapter 2 under the heading "Be Not Afraid." Jesus certainly knows that following His Way can be scary. That's why we find the phrase "be not afraid" more than twenty times in the New Testament. Yet fear grips us, particularly when we're invited to go out into the streets and seek Catholics.

Remember that the people we're evangelizing are also fearful: fearful of their brokenness, which they've pushed deep down inside them; fearful of facing a priest in confession; fearful of facing God on the Day of Judgment.

Here's the rub: fearful people can't attract fearful people. Others can sense our fear, even smell it. Joyful, fearless confidence, on the other hand, attracts fearful people, like stray sheep to a shepherd. So the first thing you need as a missionary is confidence.

How do you project confidence?

Trust in the Holy Spirit. He will guide you. Know that He is with you. You are not alone.

Above all, don't give up early. Don't miss that one soul who's waiting for you in particular. Try to avoid the "white-knuckle" approach to perseverance, which relies on you and not on the Holy Spirit. Use the Holy Spirit method: put yourself in His hands and sit back and wait for Him to make things happen. He will.

Dignity

Out on the streets, you'll see all kinds of people — angry souls, lost souls, blissfully ignorant souls. Some will be dressed in torn clothes or carrying shopping bags with all their possessions in them. Others will be dressed to the nines on their way to dinner. Still others will have barely any clothes on. Some will be hand in hand with members of the same sex. Some will have skin that's a different color from yours or will clearly have come from a faraway country.

As missionaries of Christ, we sometimes take shortcuts, out of laziness or pride or even an attempt at efficiency: "That one can't possibly be a Catholic." "No point in wasting my time on those two." "My goodness, it would be embarrassing just to be seen speaking with that one!"

These thoughts are temptations of the devil, making us doubt one of the central tenets of our Faith: we are all children of a loving God, even those of us who don't know we are or have forgotten we are or don't want to be. And if we are all children of the same God, then we are also brothers and sisters in Christ.

And we all possess a special dignity, which is the image of God within us.

So, a key disposition of the missionary must be to engage every single person we meet as a child of God, with all the dignity that that phrase implies. This missionary disposition alone can turn what could have been a very weak and uneventful encounter into a successful one.

Believing in your heart in the dignity of every person you encounter on the streets is such a key element of missionary success that I've reserved a whole chapter (chapter 12) for this topic. For now, keep dignity front and center as you seek your missionary heart and attitude.

Humility

After many years in the streets, I'm convinced that one of the greatest obstacles to missionary success is pride, both in the missionary who doesn't want to step into the gutter to fish for souls and in the potential penitents who can't overcome their pride to find a path back to God. The antidote to pride—the opposite virtue, if you will—is humility.

At least in New York, and probably in any other city in America, humility in a missionary is very disarming. In a religious context, people have come to expect the opposite: the doomsday preachers on their soap boxes in the subways, their unhappy memories of Sr. Wanda from Catholic grammar school, and sometimes even their unsettling interaction with a particularly tough priest in confession long, long ago. When instead they encounter humility in a missionary, their defenses go down quickly, and they can engage. So, as you head out into the streets, becoming humble is a key element in your missionary success.

Where can you get humility? The same place you can get all the other attitudes I've mentioned: the heart of Jesus.

Go there.

Go to Him.

He won't let you down.

∽

A willingness to answer the call, prayer and silence, reception of the sacrament of reconciliation, shared experience with Jesus, a willingness to embrace suffering, love, joy, perseverance, dignity, and humility: these are ten of the elements I see in most successful missionaries. I also know, as I mentioned earlier, that you have something no other missionary has. I don't know what it is yet, and you probably don't know either. But each of us has a unique personality—an individual set of traits, body language, and life experiences. Those things make you different from any other missionary there ever was. I've become convinced that each missionary is called for a chance meeting with maybe just one lost soul who, in some special way, can relate to and might respond only to that missionary.

Often this lost soul arrives on the scene late in the evening. Once again, perseverance is critical to success. Locked in the middle of a battle of light and darkness, a missionary is tempted repeatedly to give up, to take a break, to go home. At these moments of temptation, I remind the missionaries, "We must be getting close! Hang in there! The Holy Spirit is probably bringing a soul around the corner any minute!"

If we don't persevere on the street with joy and love in our hearts, we might go home without ever having met the soul God called us there for. Especially when the temptation to quit is highest, stay engaged! I know from experience that the soul meant for you is near.

Sometimes I put in a lot of work to hook one soul, and I don't get anywhere. Then another missionary takes over, and in five minutes, the soul I couldn't hook is off to confession. Does that mean I'm a bad missionary? No. It just means that someone else was the right missionary for that person.

I remember Angelina and her boyfriend Ricardo. I met them on Monday of Holy Week. They were both from Brazil, both "not Catholic" until they were, and both "in a hurry," but they were soon deep in conversation with me about eternity. And yet nothing I tried was quite enough to get them into the church for confession.

"It's time to let God love you, Angelina!" That was one of my best lines.

"Ricardo, Psalm 139. Let's read it." We read it. "He already knows the sins you're too embarrassed to tell the priest. He just wants you to admit to them and say you're sorry, and then give you a big hug!"

Still not enough.

"The prodigal son, Angelina! How much worse can this be?"

Slow progress being made.

Suddenly, out of the blue, another missionary, Cathy, appears on the corner. "I could see you two were deep in it, and I normally don't jump in at that point. But the Holy Spirit was prodding me."

She turns to Angelina. "Angelina, look, I have something to say to you, woman to woman. Let's go for a walk."

Off they go, Ricardo following at a distance. The couple reappears thirty minutes later, joyful and full of love.

I put a lot of work into hooking those two. But Cathy was the right missionary to bring them to shore.

∞

So, the answer to the question "Can I really be a missionary?" is yes—no matter who you are. In fact, you may be exactly the one that today's mission needs. There may be one soul waiting out there for you—someone only you can reach.

If that one soul is waiting for you, don't you think the Holy Spirit will give you what you need to get the job done? If you keep your heart linked to the heart of Jesus, you'll have the integrity and the confidence to be the missionary Jesus needs you to be.

∞

You've been praying to the heart of Jesus, making your heart His. You've been on a retreat, made a good confession, felt His mercy, and have an irrepressible urge to help others to experience the same. You've been practicing your missionary attitude in your day-to-day encounters: confidence, love, joy, perseverance, dignity, humility. You've studied your "pickup" lines, maybe tried them out on your spouse, turning a "pickup" into an encounter. You have a mission map of the parish laid out and rosaries in stock. You're ready to roll.

But what are you going to roll into?

What obstacles, arguments, and rejections are you likely to encounter on the streets? How do you respond to them?

After all, Steve (you're thinking), this "love, don't think" thing can take me only so far. How do I overcome the typical objections I'll encounter? What do I say?

First thought: read a good book from one of the great Catholic apologists of our age. Peter Kreeft's *Making Choices* comes to mind, as does Scott Hahn's *The Lamb's Supper*. And, of course, Pope Francis's *Joy of the Gospel* is a must-read. Certainly, schooling yourself in current Catholic thinking on the great issues of our time is always a good idea, particularly for a street missionary. It will help you feel more prepared to face the challenges of the street.

But you don't have to rely on just feeling prepared. You come to the mission with an attitude of joy, love, and humility. Thanks to our experience with street missions, you also come to it with a lot of practical suggestions. One of the first things you'll discover is that your success often depends not just on the fish you're trying to hook, but also on the friends and family that surround that person.

And sometimes on the dogs.

Pay attention to the dogs.

5

Friends, Family, and Dogs

St. Patrick's Old Cathedral, SoHo
—Spy Wednesday 2011

We're joined tonight in front of the church by sisters Debbie, Cathy, and Joan, three fashionable young missionaries from midtown, radiating beauty and joy.

A forty-something man from the neighborhood, out walking his dog, passes in front of the church. "Dog" is probably an understatement: the animal is nearly the size of a pony, blazing white, 120 pounds.

The sisters, who have just arrived and are very nervous about doing this street-mission stuff, bravely hail him down, hand him the schedule of liturgical services for this week, and eventually offer him the chance to receive reconciliation.

The man smiles at this suggestion, readily admitting that his last confession was when he was eight years old. "Not my thing. Anyway, time to go home and make dinner."

At that moment, all 120 pounds of the animal he was walking sits down at the sisters' feet.

"Jack, what are you doing? Come on! Time to go home for dinner!"

No movement.

"Jack, no kidding! Time to go! Up! Let's go!"

Still no movement.

The man starts frantically pulling the dog's leash, bracing his legs against the pavement as solidly as possible. No go.

Finally, the man turns to Cathy and sheepishly hands her the dog's leash. "Well, perhaps this is a sign that I should go to confession after all."

He emerges twenty minutes later beaming from the grace of the sacrament, thanks the three young ladies, and picks up the leash. The dog instantly jumps up and heads off with his friend and master.

∞

Corner of Prince and Crosby, SoHo
—Spy Wednesday 2018

A young family emerges out of the stream of pedestrians.

"Are you Catholic?" the missionary asks. "Anyone here Catholic?" The mother looks up, briefly makes eye contact with the missionary, then looks down.

"No, we're not."

"Really? You look Catholic to me."

The missionary walks with them and begins talking to the ten-year-old son. Happy little kid.

"My mom is Catholic. So am I," he proclaims.

The missionary gives him a candle to light in the church. The mother keeps walking. They catch up to her. She looks the other way and tells the missionary she's busy. She grabs the child's hand and walks off into the pedestrian river on Lafayette.

We lose her.

But maybe a seed has been planted.

Later, in the church, a twelve-year-old boy appears, alone. "I was in Catholic school until fourth grade," he says, "but my mother isn't Catholic anymore, and she pulled me out. I love this church. My parents won't come here anymore, but I like it here. I feel peaceful here."

The missionary in the back gives the boy a hug and finds a brother to speak with him. The two spend an hour together talking about God. The boy leaves later with a smile on his face.

∞

Corner of Spring and Mulberry, border of Little Italy
—Advent 2011

Under a streetlamp in SoHo, a missionary stands alone as the night grows colder and darker. A group of French tourists stroll by. "Surely I've got some Catholics here! Why not visit the cathedral? It's just three blocks away!"

A young man within the group declares firmly, "We are not Catholic!"

Already, the tidal forces of the little group are pulling the young man to the edge of the circle of light under the lamppost. In moments, he will be lost in the darkness. Barely time here for one last plea.

Turning toward the darkening group, the missionary cries, "Not Catholic? Aren't all French people Catholic? What are you then?"

Quickly, almost instinctively, the young Frenchman declares, "We are nothing."

As he speaks these words, he and the missionary lock eyes, both pondering this answer's true meaning. And then, just like that, the young man from France slips into the cold darkness.

∽

Surprisingly, of all the obstacles we encounter, friends and family are one of the biggest.

"I'd love to go in for confession, but not right now. I promised Mary here we'd go out for ice cream." "Great idea, but not right now. I'm on my way home to cook dinner for my family." "Love to, but my friends are waiting for me at a restaurant." Often, the friend or family member is with the person we're after and will insistently keep moving toward their original objective, either physically or psychologically dragging their "friend" away from a potential encounter with God. What do you do?

Over the years, we've developed several ways of turning the table on friends, making them part of the solution rather than the problem.

The first step, which should always be part of a successful encounter, is to get the person's name. Once you have a name, you can lock eyes and hold on to them and keep them engaged.

From here, a reflective question can help. "Yvette, we're talking about eternity here. Do you think your family will mind if you're fifteen minutes late?" "Don, I get it. You're rushing to a dinner reservation. But I sense you need to receive reconciliation. It won't take long. Wouldn't you rather be fifteen minutes late for dinner than miss an appointment with eternity?"

Another technique is to connect with the friend or family member who's working against you. Often we find that person is easier to turn than the soul you're targeting. "Lynn, would you like a rosary? Which color?" Then, "Lynn, do you know who God is?" And so on. Before long, Lynn will be helping you get her father or boyfriend or whomever to church.

Similar approaches can help with the friends who were initially trying to hurry along. Sometimes, we'll even turn to the friend who's tugging Jane in the wrong direction and ask her directly, "Mary, aren't you Jane's friend? Don't you want what's good for her?" More often than not, this works.

Often the friend—if it's a good friend we're dealing with— knows that her companion is suffering from something or bothered by something. And she really does want the best for her friend.

Appeal to this love and turn it over to God.

We've had many cases of non-Catholic boyfriends or girlfriends—Jews, Protestants, even agnostics—helping us get their Catholic friends into the church. Friends are powerful in a person's life, and often that power can be turned to your advantage.

Use it.

∞

St. Patrick's Old Cathedral, SoHo
—Holy Monday 2012

A cold, blustery evening in New York City. Four missionaries, two priests—that's all. Can we possibly have an impact here?

Our hit ratio seems lower than usual. Passersby are rushing to get out of the cold. We man our stations solo, at times feeling some of the loneliness of Christ on Calvary.

As the evening grows later and even colder, a jolly band of fashionably dressed young women waltz past our corner. One of the missionaries engages them.

"Not Catholic."

"In a hurry!"

"We have dinner reservations."

But one of their number looks back from the fast-moving crowd. "I'm Catholic."

"Would you like a rosary?" The missionary starts after her. "What's your name?

"Josie."

He's trotting with the group, fast heading to Mulberry Street and the darkness. "Josie, have you been to confession for Easter yet?"

"Confession? Really? I haven't been to confession in years."

"Josie, all the better. There's nothing like it. I'm sure you have something to talk about with the priest."

The little group is pulling Josie away toward the lengthening shadows of Mulberry. But the missionary is keeping pace. Memories of his failure with the young French man under the streetlamp in SoHo a year earlier still haunt him. He walks faster. He locks eyes with Josie.

"Is there really confession available right now?" Josie asks.

"Right now, Josie," the missionary responds.

"Josie!" one of the friends objects. "What are you talking about? We have a 7:30 reservation!"

"I've really got to go with my friends," Josie tells the missionary.

But the missionary doesn't give up. "Josie, I can feel that you have something to talk to the priest about. Your friends can hold the table. This is your chance."

He has her by the eyes, and he's not letting go.

"Guys," Josie says to her friends, "I'll meet you at the restaurant. I know where it is. I want to go to the church." The missionary walks her to the church, to the light ...

Later that night, as we're leaving the Mass that would end the evening, we see Josie. We're a little surprised to see her: it's 8 p.m., nearly an hour later. Josie approaches the missionary and hugs him. They lock eyes again, hers now tearful with joy.

"Thank you for being on that street corner tonight," she says. "Thank you."

∞

What is it about dogs? They often seem to be our best allies. Over the course of many missions, we've learned to make arrangements for the dogs.

"Arrangements" usually doesn't have to mean anything more than being ready to hold a leash for a while. Out in front of the church, two of our missionaries hail a man with a giant dog. When the man enters the church, one of our missionaries holds the leash for a while so the man can enjoy reconciliation. The animal is almost bigger than she is, but he sits quietly and patiently for the long wait. The man eventually emerges in tears. He needed that time—and he could have it because we were ready to deal with the dog.

Later in the evening, the man returns with his wife, who goes to confession herself. After that, the couple march down to Prince and Mott, beaming, with their giant dog in tow. Our last glimpse is of them heading into the setting sun, holding tight to the rope that holds the dog that brought them to church.

One year, our youngest missionary, five-year-old Mary, developed our best pickup line: "Can I pet your dog?"

Who could say no to that? And while Mary gets to know the dog, her mother, Jeannine, has time for a longer discussion about the Faith.

I remember another dog-related triumph vividly. As I lead an anxious soul into the church to the missionary in the back there, I notice to my left two dogs, tied up outside the courtyard, barking loudly as someone sets up the bonfire for the Easter Vigil Mass later that evening. Eddie, the parish maintenance supervisor, tries to control the anxious animals.

"Got him!" I think as we pass through the crowd. "I know those dogs. That's the guy from the parish who can't do confession because of his dogs." (A twenty-year-long problem apparently!) Later I hear the story from the missionary who reeled him in: "I told him that young Ben up there by the front gate can watch your dogs. No problem!"

"You know what?" said the wriggling fish. "They don't like people."

"Well then, tie them up in the courtyard! They'll survive. This is your last chance for confession before Easter!"

"Okay, okay, let me think about it. No, you don't need to walk me there. I'm a local. I know Msgr. Sakano."

I'm convinced that the Holy Spirit has a direct line to dogs. Spy Wednesday 2018: we see a middle-aged man out walking his dog. Fairly large animal. The missionaries on Prince and Mott invite him in for an improbable visit to the church.

"Guys, no way! Chester and I are heading home to dinner!"

"Adam" — you see, we obtained his name right away — "just for a few minutes. Light a candle for us. We're trying to make a cross of candles in there."

"Can't do it. Right, Chester? We're heading home for your favorite chopped-beef dinner!"

Chester sits down on the street corner.

Adam gives him a tug, then another.

Chester lies down. Not moving.

"Did you say someone could watch Chester for me?"

"Absolutely! We do this sort of thing all the time."

Andrew, freshly arrived from Ave Maria University for the mission, grabs the reins. Adam marches into church, candle in hand.

Man's best friend wins again.

Yet another white-dog story: our missionaries out on Lafayette are trying to evangelize a young woman who admits to "having a few Catholic friends." She's got a big white dog with her, and once again the dog sits down and won't move. Tug as she might, the woman can't get her dog up and going. A long discussion on faith ensues.

As I said, pay attention to the dogs.

∞

Children often seem to feel the pull of the Holy Spirit before their parents do. Our back-of-the-church missionary once met a mom and daughter who had come in to light candles for special intentions. They still had several churches to visit in the neighborhood—an old tradition. They tried not to make eye contact with the missionary, hoping to avoid a conversation that way.

But the missionary wouldn't quit. She started telling them about the church restoration and how much more beautiful the church would be when all the refurbishing was done.

Surprised that the beautiful church was under construction, the mom and daughter finally looked at her and asked questions. Ah! The door was opened. The Holy Spirit came rushing into their hearts.

Mom remained wary, but her daughter, Lourdes, was drawn to the offer for reconciliation and simply said, "Mom, I'm going."

That tug in her heart was strong. Never mind that it wasn't planned or that their plans had to be put aside for now.

Mom also went to confession after being assured that the priests were wonderful and that they would be delighted to receive her. What's even more beautiful is that they decided to sit patiently and pray. Mass was starting in just twenty minutes, and they decided they had time for that, too. They must have been so gloriously happy to have received the Holy Eucharist!

So, in many cases, friends and family can be your allies. Sometimes they are friends and family you'll never meet—but they affect your encounter profoundly, because they're very much present in the mind of your prospect.

Such as Patrick.

∞

St. Patrick's Old Cathedral, SoHo
—Holy Thursday 2013

In the early evening, we experience another one of those "chance" encounters. Patrick, a middle-aged man in town on business, hurries past one of our missionaries on Prince and Mott. The missionary has been seeking Catholics in a throng of two groups moving through the intersection, when he spies Patrick glancing back at him as he crosses Prince.

The missionary runs after him. A conversation follows, at first rushed, but then more measured, deeper. Patrick is a Catholic struggling to convert his non-Catholic in-laws. His wife became Catholic first, followed by her parents. The important holdout is his brother-in-law.

Just at that moment (timing is everything!), the ebullient Msgr. Sakano arrives at the corner to help, and he and the missionary convince Patrick that the best route to converting his brother-in-law might be to convert himself—to give up whatever he was rushing off to, whatever he was attached to, and to offer a long-needed confession to the Lord.

Later, Patrick comes back to the corner calm and joyful, and plots with the missionary a "conversionary trip" to Manhattan the next Sunday with his in-laws, first to Old St. Pat's for the 12:45 Easter Mass, and then to his brother-in-law's first love—art at the Met.

"Really?" says the missionary. "My wife and I give a tour at the Met called 'Man's Search for God.' I can help you with this!"

Patrick excitedly takes notes on three Baroque paintings that the missionary selects to help him stir the brother-in-law's spirit. As Patrick prepares to depart, the missionary asks him his brother-in-law's name.

"Adam," he says.

The missionary and Patrick both draw in a breath at that, and in each other's eyes they read the significance of that name and this mission.

"Adam," Patrick repeats firmly. "I'm going to bring back Adam."

Yes. Friends and family — and dogs — can be unexpectedly important to reeling in the souls you're fishing for.

But some of those souls — to be honest, a lot of them — may be afraid to go to confession. "I'm just not ready," they might say.

How do you deal with that reluctance? What can you do to get your prospect through that last barrier and in to see the priest?

6

"I'm Not Ready for Confession Yet"

St. Patrick's Old Cathedral, SoHo
—Good Friday 2017

During and immediately after the *Via Crucis*—the annual Way of the Cross procession in the neighborhood—our business on Prince and Mott goes into hyperdrive. Despite having armed ourselves with two bags of rosaries, we've already had to rush a missionary back to headquarters for more supplies. (I later discovered that the "missionary" we sent on this errand was a local newspaper reporter sent to write a story about all the commotion down in SoHo. Oops!)

A young, fashionably dressed couple approach us at the corner, on their way out of the church. "No, thank you. We just came from church, and someone there already gave us rosaries. We're all set."

"Terrific!" says the missionary with a joyful smile. "So you went to confession too?"

"Oh, no, not confession. Neither of us is ready for that!" A long discussion leads to Psalm 139.

"The Lord already knows everything you did," the missionary says. "He just wants you to come in and make up with Him—for you to apologize so He can give you a big hug."

Anna has "nothing to confess." She's firm on this. "One of the missionaries in the back of the church already asked us."

"Well, I have something to confess," says Joey firmly. "I'd like to go."

"Come on, Joey, You're fine. You don't have anything to confess. Let's go."

Back to Psalm 139.

Joey says, "I will go."

Together, the couple and the missionary walk toward the church. The missionary gives Anna a pamphlet on preparing for confession—"Just in case you need something to read while you're waiting for Joey here."

They arrive at the gate, but Joey stops.

"I need to get ready, to collect my thoughts. I'm not ready to go in. I promise you I will go. I promise."

Sensing that he has taken this as far as he can, the missionary leaves them there, in the hands of the Holy Spirit.

Eventually, Joey musters the courage to reenter the church.

The missionary at the back of the church sees the couple with their reconciliation pamphlet in hand and knows that the missionaries on Prince and Mott have gone deep here but need help.

"Welcome back!" she says. "Are you guys thinking of going to confession? I have wonderful missionary priests here."

"Yes, we're thinking about it, but we're not quite sure how to do it."

"Let's pray on this together."

The missionary kneels behind them in a pew and begins meditating out loud. "Did I miss Sunday Mass?... Did I say something bad about someone?... Did I lose my temper?... Did I look at pictures on the Internet that I shouldn't have?"

About an hour later, Joey and Anna arrive back at Prince and Mott for the third time, now joyful and glowing. "We did it! We did it! Thank you so much. We feel so great!"

As they head off into the early evening dusk, the missionary reflects on how many missionaries it took to help that couple back to God: the fifty-some-odd teens witnessing the Way of the Cross through the neighborhood; the missionaries on Prince and Mott who twice sent them into the church; the missionary in the back of the church who prepared them; the priests who heard their confessions; and the Holy Spirit, who moved them and ultimately embraced them. The team at work.

Later, in his sermon at the 3:00 service in the basilica, Msgr. Sakano talks about how this most solemn of days became "Good" Friday instead of "Bad" Friday or "Tragic" Friday. We know that through the Cross He saved us, sinners all: Peter. John. You. Me.

Through His ultimate sacrifice, He transformed us from sinners into saints. He turned bad to good. Hate to love. Gloom to joy.

∞

This experience of Christ's mercy and love is unique to the sacrament of reconciliation. But for too many Catholics, it has been lost.

In parishes, the sacrament is often relegated to a scheduled appointment, which carries an aura of gravity that often puts us off rather than encourages us. Or it's a brief, once-a-week, thirty-minute interlude before the Saturday vigil Mass, which creates a time deadline discouraging deep discourse with God.

Little sins, unforgiven, have a way of piling up into bigger sins, still unforgiven. In self-defense, we begin to rationalize the sin away, but in doing so, we build a bigger and bigger wall between us and Christ. We stop praying. We no longer hear his voice. Our New York City mission, above all else, is a direct attempt to help our brothers and sisters in Christ break down that wall and let His love and mercy back in.

That's why we make the sacrament of reconciliation the cornerstone of our mission. Yes, it can be hard to overcome years of built-up resistance. Catholics can be genuinely afraid of confession. They may have had a bad experience years ago with an unsympathetic priest. They may be afraid to face their own demons. They may be afraid they'll have to give up sinful habits they don't want to give up. Or they may just be afraid of embarrassing themselves in front of the priest—and that might be the worst fear of all.

∞

"I'm too embarrassed to tell the priest" is one of the most common responses we hear.

Let's face it: to the average human, the idea of admitting to another human that you've done something that's embarrassing or shameful is very difficult. This difficulty is what lies behind many Catholics' resistance to the sacrament of confession.

It's also a difficulty highlighted for them by the devil, who knows that if he can keep a soul out of the merciful hands of God, he can then begin to work on that soul's conscience, gradually weakening and eventually killing it. First, it's "Well, that's too embarrassing to tell the priest." Then it's, "Well, everyone's doing this. It's really not so bad." Finally it's, "What was I so worried about? That behavior isn't sinful. In fact, there really isn't such a thing as sin!"

This is what we call the "slippery slope of sin." Near the bottom of this slope is a deeply mortal sin, one that even a lost soul will know is evil, but at this stage, he has also been led to believe that he's unforgivable (see the next chapter).

Depending on the person we're speaking with and how the Holy Spirit may be guiding us at the time, we've used several successful lines of attack to deal with embarrassed souls who feel that they can't talk to the priest.

- *Highlight the opportunity.* We have priests right now. If you wait, you'll forget, or you'll be busy. You'll never have a better chance than now.
- *Describe how good it feels.* God wants to give you a big hug. You'll feel so good when you've done it. At Easter Sunday Mass, you'll experience the joy of the Resurrection in a very personal way!
- *Emphasize Jesus' sacrifice for our sins.* Jesus suffered so that you could be forgiven. All you must endure is a little embarrassment. Do it for Jesus.
- *Remind them that they're not really talking to the priest at all,* but to Jesus *through* the priest. In theological terms, the priest is there *in persona Christi*—"in the person of Christ." When Catholics start realizing that confession is really a chance to talk to God directly, it changes their perspective. After all, God already knows what you've done! Nothing to be embarrassed about that you aren't already embarrassed about!
- *Use images and Bible stories people can identify with.* One of my favorites is Georges de La Tour's *The Penitent Magdalen* (look it up on the Internet if you'd like). In speaking of this lovely painting, I remind the person that in confession we encounter the deep power of the Lord's forgiveness, deep enough to have gotten through to a woman who had done it all—and went on, with the Lord's mercy, to become a saint. Another good story of forgiveness is that of St. Peter. What can be worse than

denying Christ, not once but three times? But Peter didn't sulk or self-confess his sin. He jumped out of the boat on the Sea of Galilee and swam with his clothes on to get to Jesus and receive reconciliation. And he became the leader of the Church. In Caravaggio's *The Denial of Peter*, the furrowed brow of Peter says everything about the pain of a soul who has denied Christ.

• *Describe God's boundless mercy.* Some of the psalms were written by a repentant sinner: David, who committed adultery with his general's wife, had a child out of wedlock, and then arranged the general's murder to cover up his crime! These psalms are very effective confession preps, even on the streets of New York. As mentioned previously, Psalm 139 is one of my favorite psalms for describing the sacrament of confession to Catholics who feel that it's embarrassing and unendurable. Speaking to God, the psalmist says, "You know when I sit and stand; you understand my thoughts from afar. You sift through my travels and my rest; with all my ways you are familiar" (vv. 1–2). We use this psalm on the back of a prayer card of Rembrandt's masterpiece of mercy, *The Return of the Prodigal Son*. As we read Psalm 139 together, a deep truth often begins to dawn on the person we're talking to: God already knows what you did, so it's way too late to be embarrassed about it. All He wants is for you to admit it, say you're sorry, and make up. Then He puts His big arms around you and gives you a God-sized hug. He just wants to be your friend again.

• *Emphasize Jesus' love for them.* Love is an appealing virtue, and when people hear the sacrament of confession described as the sacrament of love, they see it differently.

"Jesus loves you. Reconciliation is His way of showing you His mercy and His love. Let Him love you."

• *Tell them the story of St. Jerome.* St. Jerome devoted his life to God, to translating the Bible from Greek to Latin. But near the end of his life, Jerome was praying in church and heard the voice of God: "Jerome, I want something more from you." You can imagine how Jerome felt. "More? Are you kidding? I just spent my entire life on your Word!" "Yes, Jerome. But I need something more. I need the one thing that is keeping you from me. I want your sins." So even "good people" need the sacrament of confession to grow closer to God.

• *Ask them to go to confession for their mother (or father).* Many Catholics remember fondly the devoted, loving, yet firm hand of their parents as they raised them in the Faith and being taken by them to church for the sacrament of penance. They know how proud Mom will be when they tell her on Easter Sunday that they went to confession in New York at Old St. Pat's, or how happy Dad will be up in heaven watching them. Appeal to the roots of their faith.

• *Give them the basics on how to make a confession.* For today's Catholics, many of whom have not been to confession in years, their embarrassment about talking to a priest is often rooted in a much simpler problem: not knowing how to make a good confession. For Catholics who have been away from the sacrament for a long time, forgetting the Act of Contrition or lacking a list of sinful behaviors for a self-examination can be an obstacle in itself. We always keep on hand a pamphlet called *A Guide to the Sacrament of Confession*, and we sometimes give a copy to those who seem ready for it. We assure souls who seem overwhelmed that the priest will guide them through or that the missionary in the back of the church will prepare them. Just make sure that your priests in the confessionals are prepared for this; if they've been hearing only the confessions of the "regulars" they may be caught off guard!

∞

St. Patrick's Old Cathedral, SoHo
—Holy Thursday 2016

The missionary in the back of the church meets a couple from Florida "just in to pray for a few minutes," not interested at all in confession.

But she senses they're deeply troubled.

Eventually, the husband agrees to see a priest. And he's in there for a long time.

After a while, the wife begins crying. Soon she's sobbing uncontrollably.

"What's wrong, Mary?" the missionary asks. "He's telling the priest everything!"

"That's the beauty of this sacrament," the missionary tells Mary. "You can tell God everything, without reservation. You can unburden your heart. You can be transformed."

When her husband leaves the confessional, Mary goes in.

∞

Times Square
—Good Friday 2017

Our missionary Chris and his team reach out to a woman from the theater district, in costume, seemingly on her happy way, waltzing along in her disguise. She gives them a simple prayer request and moves on. About fifteen minutes later, she returns to talk to two of the young women, Nicole and Maria, from Chris's group, now alone.

"Oh, I'm so glad I caught up to you girls. I have something to confess to you."

"We're here for you. Tell us."

"Well, I gave that nice young man with you a kind of fake prayer intention, something that would seem normal. I was too embarrassed to give him my real one."

"No prayer is too embarrassing for God. He wants your prayers, your deepest ones especially. 'Ask and you shall receive.' You can tell us."

She begins to tear up. Nicole hugs her. Maria embraces her. The prayer comes forward. Tears flow. The three women are now standing on the corner, hugging.

"Let's all pray together right here for your intention," says Nicole.

"Right now? Right here on the corner?"

"Yes. Right here."

They form a small circle, holding hands, and Maria leads the group in prayer. The actress, shedding layers of hiddenness as the prayer goes on, sobs uncontrollably.

As they part ways later, the woman seems at peace. "I really needed you girls. I really needed you."

The right missionary in the right place at the right time can overcome any reluctance. That's why, as always, perseverance is essential. That one soul you were meant to find may be coming around the corner right now.

Or the one you thought you had just missed may be coming back to give you another chance.

∞

It's later the same Good Friday, back at the church. Jim comes in. Jeannine's crew out on Lafayette had met him Wednesday night, but he thought it was too late for him. "I can't go to confession! It's been many, many years. I have so many sins. Where would I begin?"

"Jim," Jeannine said, "don't get paralyzed about where to begin. Just begin. God is waiting for you like a loving father."

Together, they walked and talked all the way to the cathedral, about five blocks away. Jim was melting but not quite there.

Finally, outside the church, he slipped away. "I need to think about this, Jeannine. Give me some time. I promise I'll come back tomorrow."

Jeannine backed off, trusting in the Holy Spirit and the power of their prayers. But as Jim walked away into the night, "I knew I'd found that one soul I was meant to meet," Jeannine told us later. "I prayed for him that night and the next morning."

Jim didn't show up on Thursday. Even so, Jeannine didn't stop praying.

Now here he is at last, and this time he has come as far as the back of the church.

The missionary in the back approaches him.

"I'm thinking about it," Jim says. "I'm just not ready." He prays for a while, then gets up to leave.

The missionary stops him. "Jim," she says, "do you know about St. Jerome?"

Jim listens intently to the story. Then he turns back into the church.

After receiving reconciliation, just before the 3:00 service begins, he finds both of the missionaries who brought him back. Now he has a huge smile on his face.

"I did it, Jeannine! I did it! Thank you, thank you for helping me. I feel so free!"

"Jim," Jeannine says, "each of us was called here to this mission to find one soul. I just know you were the soul I was meant to find."

But the day is not over. Well into the evening souls are still coming in. At 7:44 Francesco approaches us, full of joy.

"I did it! I did it! I feel so light, like a great burden has been lifted from my back! And it's all because of Bob here." He points to the missionary who brought him in. "That man saved me."

"Tell me more," says the other missionary.

"Well, I was walking down Prince. I walk past this church all the time, and I'm used to seeing you missionaries out here on Good Friday. So I always cross to the other side to avoid you. But this time, I'm not sure why, I didn't do that. Bob stopped me. He talked with me a long time about letting myself be loved on Good Friday. Finally, I promised him I'd return after I got my hair cut. He accepted my promise to come back. And in the barber shop I kept thinking about that—about how many times in my life I didn't live up to a promise and how I was about to do that again. Then I remembered what Bob said about letting myself be loved, about becoming the better person God wants me to be. And I decided, 'Not this time! This time I am going to live up to my word. I'm going back.' And I did. Now a ton of bricks is off my back. I'm done with the lying, the cheating, the drugs. It's over. I'm on a new course. I literally feel like the prodigal son. I was lost. Now I'm found."

∽

These were just ordinary Catholics with ordinary problems, and they still had to overcome a lot of fear and reluctance to get to confession.

But sometimes we meet someone who's in much worse shape than that. There are Catholics out there who really think God could never take them back. What do you do when you run across someone who really believes that there's one sin in his life that God will never forgive?

7

That Unforgivable Sin

St. Patrick's Old Cathedral, SoHo
— Holy Monday 2015

Ann, a young woman rushing off to somewhere, crosses the path of one of our missionaries on Prince and Mott. Although initially in a hurry, she pauses long enough to get a rosary and a schedule of services.

The ensuing conversation reveals someone in deep pain who feels as if there's no way she could ask for the Lord's mercy in confession after a long, long time away. No way.

The missionary pulls out this year's secret weapon — a prayer card of Rembrandt's masterpiece *The Return of the Prodigal Son*.

"Ann, based on what you're telling me, you're not the prodigal son, but rather, the older son. On the surface, he was in line, but underneath he just couldn't get on his knees and ask for God's love. He was outside the feast. That's where you are right now. Outside the feast."

An hour later, she returns from the church joyful, on a new course. "Thank you! Thank you for being on that street corner tonight!"

∞

The unforgiven, "unforgivable" sin is one obstacle that our missionaries face but rarely talk about. Often this is something so mortal that even a secularized Catholic knows it's bad. That knowledge is a good thing, but when the Catholic believes that his sin can never be forgiven, we have a problem.

Many times, in the case of young women, it will be an abortion. Although most women will not openly talk about a past abortion in a street encounter, if you've locked eyes with a mother who has destroyed her child, you can read her pain. As she thinks about it without saying it, she often involuntarily wells up with tears.

Other similarly deep, unforgiven sins might be felony crimes or murder, extramarital affairs, or a permanent break after a violent argument with a parent or an adult child.

In all these instances, it's very important for you to be engaged at an emotional level with the person, and to be very gentle. Questions or reflective responses are better than statements or entreaties. If you give them the proper encouragement, these troubled souls will do most of the talking that needs to happen to lead them to the church.

Understand that most of these souls who believe they've committed an unforgivable sin unknowingly suffer more from pride than from anything else. They believe their sin is even greater than God's mercy. In effect, they believe they're greater than God. Although they never articulate their problem this way, sometimes the first step in bringing them back is to help them see that this is what they're really saying. From this perspective, people can begin to see that no sin can ever really be unforgivable.

Encounters with souls in deep pain can be very time-consuming and difficult. Sometimes it may seem impossible to bring them to an immediately successful conclusion. But these are the encounters that missionaries are most needed for. Souls who have committed a sin so bad that even they realize it was terrible are often inconsolable, and therefore in despair. They believe that they are already at the bottom of the slippery slope and heading to perdition. Like a smoker whose lungs are clogged and breath shortened, their spiritual lungs are hardened from lack of spiritual air. They're slowly suffocating. For these souls, the power of being invited back by a gentle, loving, joyful Catholic is quite tangible. It may be their only route back.

So persevere! Even if you don't succeed, you will at least have peeled off a very thick layer of armor and planted the thought in their minds that, yes, their sins might be forgivable.

And if you need another motivation to persevere, just imagine the scene after you succeed. Invariably, the most difficult cases — the ones you must work hard at reeling in — break down when they come back out of the church after confession. They're joyful and light on their feet, amazed that this heavy burden they've been carrying around for ten, twenty, even forty years is suddenly lifted. They come back to find you on the street and give you one of the biggest, most joyful bear hugs you've ever received.

This is the street-missionary equivalent of winning the jackpot. And it's moments like this that you feel, really and truly, the supporting presence of the Holy Spirit beside you, whispering in your ear, "We did it! We did it!"

As noted earlier, we often keep in our pockets custom-made prayer cards with a painting from the Metropolitan Museum on the front and a psalm on the back. Three of our favorite cards for people with "unforgivable" sins are Jean-Antoine Watteau's *Mezzetin* with Lamentations 3:17–20 on the back, Rembrandt's *Return of the Prodigal Son* with Psalm 139, and Georges de La Tour's *Penitent Magdalen* with Psalm 27.

∞

Mulberry and Broome, Little Italy
—Holy Thursday 2016

Our team out in Little Italy finds Michael, sixty years old and "not Catholic."

But our teenage missionary senses something deeper happening. He engages Michael in discussion. "Would you like to visit the church and pray?"

"What are you doing out here?"

"We're missionaries."

"Missionaries! Why don't you go mission out in the Middle East, where they need you?"

"We're needed here. This city needs Jesus too. It needs His love."

"Okay, I was Catholic. But I can't go into a church. They'll never forgive me. I married outside the Church. I'm done for, not worthy, a sinner all my life. Haven't been back in forty years."

Tim assures him that he is misinformed terribly. Quite the opposite: the Lord still loves him and wants him back. The Church wants him back. Every sin can be forgiven—you must only ask. "Jesus wants to recapture you out here in the streets. He wants to love you. He wants you to come home."

Later, one of the adult missionaries with the group, B.J., walks Michael in from Little Italy and stays with him right up to the entrance to the confessional, preparing him for the gift he is about to receive. A new beginning. The first step of a long journey. From sinner to saint.

Later, during a powerful homily on the transformative power of the sacraments, Msgr. Sakano speaks of Christ's call for sinners, those who think they're not worthy and not able to carry His cause into the streets.

"This unworthiness is precisely what qualifies them for the task. Their unworthiness gives them the gift of humility needed to receive His grace fully in the sacraments, and through that grace to be transformed from sinners to saints, from ragged followers to inspired apostles, from humdrum observers to impassioned missionaries."

∞

We don't always overcome the "unforgivable" sinner's reluctance right away. But even when we don't, we may still be bearing the message that that one special soul needs to hear.

∞

Mission Headquarters, Mulberry Street
Holy Saturday 2017

Near the end of the night, our Cheshire team has assembled in headquarters, telling us about their experiences on the streets before the long bus ride home. Collette, a gentle, soft-spoken missionary and a devoted mother, tells a story from outside the abortion clinic.

"It's pretty quiet. We're praying the rosary. A young woman walks slowly out of the clinic. She seems deep in thought.

"'Are you okay?'

"'Yes, I'll be fine, thank you.'

"'Are you sure?'

"'Yes.'

"But I could tell she wasn't fine at all. A mother knows these things. This woman was deeply troubled. So I asked her, 'Would you like a rosary? You can pray to our Blessed Mother with this. It was blessed at the old cathedral by Msgr. Sakano.'

" 'Oh, thank you. That would be nice.'

" 'Would you like to come to our Mass tonight?'

"She had a strong reaction to that: 'Oh, no. I couldn't. And I shouldn't.'

"Of course you can. Of course you should! Our doors are open to you. God still loves you, no matter what. You are His precious daughter, and He will never give up on you. Never. No matter what you've done. He wants you back."

"She gave me a hug, and she took a rosary. And then she slipped away. But one of our other missionaries saw her around the corner: she paused, she leaned against the wall, and then, she started to cry."

Minutes before the Cheshire team leaves, Fr. Simon leads them all in a final prayer of thanks. They're standing in a circle, holding hands. Another missionary is with them. He's crying tears of joy. It's been a long, emotion-filled week, and he briefly breaks down.

"All week long, I've been sending small teams up to that abortion clinic. All week. It's a dark corner — there seems to be an evil presence there — and very few people pass there. I was really getting ready to give up, thinking it's not fair to send a new team there, wondering whether the Holy Spirit really wants us there, wondering whether it's a good use of our limited missionary resources. But when your team volunteered to go, it gave me the courage to give it one more shot."

He looks at Collette and continues: "Tonight my self-doubts have been answered. I believe that each one of us is called to this mission for a special purpose — that each of us has some special talent or disposition that's particularly suited to some soul out there in the streets. And I believe the Holy Spirit brings that person to us. Collette, you answered the call. You took the tough assignment. And you were there for that young woman at just the right moment, giving her the hug and the reassurance she needed to go on. You were just the gentle mother she needed at that very difficult time. What if you hadn't been there?"

Even if you don't bring that soul into the church right now, you've made a difference. Sometimes you don't even get to speak to the soul who needs you, and yet you still need to remember that you have a way of making a difference.

∞

Another story comes from the same group of missionaries, which included brothers from the Cheshire seminary. They're across the corner from the abortion clinic, and silently they walk back and forth, praying the Rosary, surrounding the clinic with prayer.

After a while, two young women emerge. One is sobbing uncontrollably; the other is trying to comfort her.

The brothers keep praying. Somehow they feel a connection to this young woman. She seems aware of their presence but doesn't engage them.

Then a young man pulls up in a car. The two women climb in and drive off into the darkness. The moment passes.

Praying was all our team could do. But we knew that that praying was a success too.

∞

San Gennaro Mission, Mulberry Street
— September 2016

About halfway through the evening, one of our missionaries meets Ricardo. He's Catholic and gladly takes a rosary.

"No time, though, for going into the church to light a candle," he says. "On my way home for an appointment."

"Have you been inside the church lately, Ricardo?" our missionary asks.

"Of course. I go to Mass every Sunday."

"Fantastic! That's great! Why not come in for a couple of minutes to light a candle?"

Ricardo's in a hurry. He has no time. But the missionary can feel that he's also disturbed by something. The discussion goes on.

"What have you been up to lately, Ricardo?"

"Trying to get my life back together."

"Hmm. From what?"

Now he's talking as if he's forgotten his urgent appointment. Ricardo is a former operations manager from a prominent New York company. He's a college graduate. He "was making six figures until the bottom dropped out." Now he's sliding down fast. He has lost his job. Legal action. Depression. Despair. Drugs. Addiction.

"And one other thing," he adds. "That was a white lie I told you. I haven't been to Mass much lately."

"Ricardo, that was more than a white lie. Not coming to Mass is saying no to God. It's cutting yourself off from Him and the graces He offers. It's mortal. It's not a small white lie."

Silence.

Their eyes connect. More silence.

"I feel like Job," Ricardo says at last. "I had it all, and now I've been brought low."

"Ricardo, feeling like Job is okay. Job stayed faithful to God through all his sufferings. And he got back on top in the end. He was restored."

"That's what I need to do," says Ricardo. "Stay faithful."

"Ricardo, come in to light a candle. Put your prayers before Jesus."

"I'm in a hurry."

"You told me that thirty minutes ago, Ricardo. By now you could have been in and out of the church, with your prayers front and center up there on the altar!"

The discussion continues; Ricardo is really hurting. The missionary begins to wonder whether he's doing the right thing. People are streaming by at thirty souls a minute. Is he missing that one soul who really needs him to be there? But he feels drawn to Ricardo. He feels a need to help this one soul get back. He stays with him. He implores him. He listens to him. He loves him.

Gradually, patiently, he leads Ricardo toward the church, candle and rosary in hand. They hug outside the church, and Ricardo walks in confidently.

Later, one of the missionaries in the back of the church, and the Holy Spirit, guide him to confession and grace.

He's restored.

Job no longer.

∽

St. Patrick's Old Cathedral, SoHo
—Tuesday of Holy Week 2017

Erica, from the faraway foreign country of California, comes back to the corner after finally going into the church.

"Wow! I feel so much better! It's been years since I went to confession. I can't believe I was so worried about it. I feel so much lighter, happier, more joyful! Thank you for stopping me. The world has gotten so secular, and I realize my faith is so beautiful in comparison. I really have to go deeper."

Together, she and the missionary reflect on John 21. "Peter is discouraged," the missionary says. "He is in a state of sin for denying Jesus three times. It's weighing him down. He doesn't feel right. So he decides to go fishing. Is he giving up or just distracting himself? That's something we all tend to do, Erica! John, his beloved friend, sticks with him, looking for his chance to bring Peter home. John, not Peter, is the one who recognizes Christ on the shore. When Peter hears John call out, 'It's the Lord!', Peter, who still can't recognize Jesus—but trusts John—jumps overboard to his God. He reconciles with Him. A weight has been lifted. He goes out into deep water. He builds the Church."

"That's me!" Erica says. "That's me!"

We never give up on a Catholic who thinks he has an unforgivable sin. That doesn't mean we get everyone into the confessional. But it's surprising how often we succeed. When we don't succeed right away, we pray. We didn't bring in that soul this time, but we may have planted a seed. The rest is in the hands of the Holy Spirit.

What about the ones who have broken with the Church completely?

How do we approach the ones who insist that they're done with being Catholic?

8

Bringing Back Lapsed Catholics

St. Patrick's Old Cathedral, SoHo
—Monday of Holy Week 2014

It's near closing time. Bob is already late for dinner, but he decides to wait at his post for one last soul.

It doesn't take long. In just a minute or two, a woman comes along who at first says she's not Catholic. After a few more questions, she says she went to Our Lady of Sorrows school and then to a Catholic high school. Her mom was Catholic, and her father was Pentecostal. There was a lot of conflict between the two, so she grew up confused spiritually.

"Give me two minutes to explain," Bob counters. He talks about our innate desire to love and be loved.

Soon she's crying. She's "having a very difficult time right now," she says, and she can't believe how coincidental it is that they're talking about this. "I feel so bad that when things were going fine I didn't turn to God. Now that I'm having trouble, I'm turning to Him. It seems very hypocritical."

"Don't worry about it. In all situations, God tries to draw us close to Him, sometimes more effectively than others. In the end, all that matters to God is that we're close to Him."

Bob walks her into the church, the last soul of the evening.

THE MISSIONARY OF WALL STREET

∞

People fall away from the Church for all sorts of reasons. Sometimes they rebelled when they were young: they rejected the Church because they were rejecting their parents and everything their parents made them do. Going to Mass was part of the package.

They might have made some life decision they knew the Church didn't approve of—living with someone without marrying, for example.

In some cases, they might just have drifted away. They never made a conscious decision to leave, but after years of no involvement with the Church, they've stopped thinking of themselves as Catholic. Or they're still "culturally" Catholic, but "not practicing."

Most of these people have one thing in common: they think the Church doesn't want them back. They think they've been away so long that the Church has rejected them. Or they think it would take so much work to get back into the Church's good graces that they shrink from the prospect.

Meanwhile, they've been missing the joy and strength that can come only from the sacraments. They may not recognize what's missing, but they know something is wrong in their lives. They just can't get over the barriers that keep them out of the Church.

So, how do we bring them back?

Often the answer is amazingly simple: we just *invite* them back.

Our experience on the streets is that many of these souls are sad or perhaps even in despair but don't know how to get back on track. They've been away from the sacrament of confession for too long.

So they avoid it.

They stay lost.

But deep inside, they're hoping they'll be found.

∞

Prince and Mott, SoHo
—*Good Friday 2018*

Our missionary spots a young woman who has been coming right toward him, then suddenly cuts left, attempting to jaywalk to the other side of Mott without going through the corner where the missionaries are standing. But the light on Prince is green, and she's forced to wait a moment while the traffic passes.

The missionary approaches her: "Excuse me, miss. You look Catholic."

"Yes, I am."

"Would you like a rosary?"

"Okay, thank you."

"How about a service schedule for Easter?"

"Why not?" She takes it.

"By the way, have you had a chance to get your Easter confession in yet?"

A nervous laugh. "Well, not yet."

A long conversation follows. The woman, Alex, hasn't been to confession in over a decade. She's in a hurry. But something is holding her here at Prince and Mott.

The pull of God.

She feels it.

The missionary is sure she feels it.

"Alex, have you ever had a chance to go to Mass on Easter Sunday right after you've been to confession? You feel like you're resurrecting with Christ! You feel like newly fallen snow! You feel incredible joy, like you've never felt before. You feel like the apostle John must have felt when he looked into the tomb and realized that the Lord had risen."

More talk.

"Do you really think I can go?" she asks. "I don't even know how to do a confession anymore."

"Alex, that's not an issue. The Lord wants you back. His priest will guide you through your confession. You just have to say yes."

Forty minutes later, the missionary is engaged with another couple. Alex approaches the corner and waits patiently.

Finally, the couple go on their way.

Alex comes over to the missionary and hugs him, with joy in her eyes.

"Alex," the missionary says, "you have on what we call the 'confession glow.'"

"I do!" she replies. "I did it! And you were right. I feel so good! I'm so happy you stopped me. I was trying to avoid you. Now I feel healed."

∞

Outside the cupcake shop, SoHo
—Monday of Holy Week 2016

A missionary is spending a long time here with a fifty-year-old man who says he hasn't been to confession in thirty years.

"I've seen worse," the missionary replies encouragingly.

"My wife is very anti-Catholic.... The kids have no interest. I wish I could fix this."

"He can help you."

Silence.

"John, what's wrong here? You look worried."

"I just got some bad news. Real bad."

Quiet.

"You have to take the first step, John. You have to ask for His love."

John is still deep in thought. He wants to go into that church, but something is holding him back.

Then, from behind the missionary, a voice on the bench in front of the store: "Let's go, John! This has gone far enough. We've got to get home for dinner."

The wife! There the whole time!

John abruptly departs, hurrying off with his wife into the dusk. We never get an "I'll be back."

But we pray that he'll be back anyway.

Sometimes we have to be satisfied with planting a seed.

∞

Prince and Mott, SoHo
—Holy Saturday 2018

Dick and his son, visiting New York from the Midwest, spend twenty minutes with Bob talking about the importance of confession, its transformative power, the grace it gives us to be the people God wants us to be. Sinners to saints.

Finally, the two head in nervously.

It's Dick's first confession in sixty-two years.

Forty minutes later, they're back, beaming.

"That was so beautiful. So beautiful. I can't believe I waited sixty-two years to do this. Thank you, thank you, thank you!"

Now they don't seem to want to leave the corner of Prince and Mott.

"I wish we could stay right here," Dick says. "I wish you guys were my neighbors."

"We are now, Dick. We're all neighbors now."

THE MISSIONARY OF WALL STREET

∞

St. Patrick's Old Cathedral, SoHo
—Monday of Holy Week 2018

It's about 5:00, and Fr. Stephen arrives at the back of the church. He sees Marie, filling in for the missionary who is usually stationed there. "Marie, I saw a woman begging at the 6 train exit up on Bleecker. Why don't you invite her to the church for confession?"

I'm in the church watching this conversation, and I'm thinking it's a lost cause. I've passed that woman many times. I've talked with her. Never—not once—have I gotten her to show any interest in confession.

But Marie heads out.

Ten minutes later, there she is, with Julie, the woman from the subway exit, coming into the church. Julie has her first confession in decades. Another soul's course turned.

From experiences like this, I learn never to give up. Just because I wasn't the right missionary for some soul doesn't mean that soul can't be reached. Sometimes it just takes a different perspective, a different approach, a different missionary.

∞

All these souls knew something about the Catholic Church and had had some relationship in the past. But there are many people out there who have no relationship with any institutional religion at all. They usually recognize a spiritual dimension in life, but they think they can approach it in their own way, on their own terms. Why do they need anyone to get between them and God?

We see more and more of these people on the streets. How can we approach people who insist that they're "spiritual but not religious"?

9

"I Have My Own Relationship with God"

Prince and Mott, SoHo
—Spy Wednesday 2010

Our missionary approaches the corner just as Bob hails a middle-aged businessman rushing past.

"Are you Catholic?"

"Been there, done that!" the man barks. He presses on.

Somehow the missionary's timing is perfect. He steps onto the sidewalk, right into the man's path. "What do you mean, 'Been there, done that'?"

The man is in a hurry, so the missionary starts walking with him.

"Forty years ago, I was a good Catholic. Went to Mass every Sunday. Then, one day at Mass, it occurred to me that the whole liturgy thing is completely a human fabrication. Made up. And if it's fake, well, then so is the Catholic Church. I haven't been in a church since. So now I have no relationship with organized religion, and I sort of work things out on my own. I have my own relationship with God. I don't need you people."

"How's your relationship going?"

"Not very good, to be honest. I'm starting to wonder if He even exists.... Now, if you don't mind, I'm in a bit of a hurry. Trying to get back to my hotel to pack my bags and get to the airport."

"Why? Are you leaving town?"

"Yes, I'm leaving town, hopefully for good. I'm from Canada. I just came down to settle some family business."

"What's your name?"

"Rich."

"Rich, what else besides business have you been doing in New York?"

"Not much. Went to the Met on Sunday."

"Really? What did you see there?"

"Not much of interest. I stayed mostly in the European painting section. Saw a painting about something called 'Emmaus' that seemed interesting, but I couldn't figure it out."

Ding! Ding! Ding! Bells go off in the missionary's head. He and his wife have been developing a tour at the Met on man's relationship with God, and just two weeks earlier they had spent the better part of an hour finding, and then studying, this very painting. How Rich stumbled onto it is a mystery. At that time, it was way off the beaten track in the Met; with maps, it took the missionary almost twenty minutes just to find it.

But what's more incredible is what the painting is about.

"Rich, that's crazy! You were at the Met and somehow found that seventeenth-century masterpiece by Diego Velázquez, *The Supper at Emmaus*. I just recently spent an afternoon studying that painting. Can you give me a moment to tell you what it's about? It's kind of related to your issue with the Catholic Church."

By now, Rich has stopped walking. He and the missionary are nose to nose by the old brick wall around Old St. Pat's, down near Prince and Mulberry.

"Try me," Rich says.

"Well, Rich, that painting was painted during the Counter-Reformation and was partly intended to counter Protestant charges that the liturgy of the Mass was a fabrication by deluded human beings."

"Really? Come on."

The missionary tells Rich the story from Luke's Gospel of the road to Emmaus, and the supper that followed (Luke 24:13–35). "It's Easter Sunday. Two discouraged disciples have thrown in the towel. They had thought they had found the Messiah, but then He was killed on a cross. Now they're leaving Jerusalem in despair. A man appears. They don't recognize Him, but He follows along with them, citing passages from the Jewish Scriptures, our Old Testament, and explaining how those passages prophesied the Passion of their Teacher. The disciples' eyes begin to open. By the time they reach their destination, their 'hearts burning within them,' they invite the stranger to dine with them. He agrees. And over the meal, as He says the blessing, their eyes are opened. They see that the stranger is Jesus, the risen Lord. Overjoyed, they become some of the first evangelists, running all the way back to the Upper Room to announce the Lord's Resurrection to their brothers."

The missionary brings it back to the painting. "And that's what Velázquez's masterpiece is about. It depicts the single moment when the two disciples suddenly recognize Christ. They're literally jumping for joy, right off the canvas! Rich, don't you see? This is the story of the first Mass after the Resurrection. Christ Himself offered it. On the walk was the Liturgy of the Word, the reading of the Old Testament, and the New Testament story that's related to it. At supper was the Liturgy of the Eucharist, the offering of the bread and wine, now blessed and transubstantiated into the Body and Blood of Christ. Your disbelief in the Mass and the Church is addressed directly by this Gospel passage from Luke, and by Velazquez's incredible painting of it!

You saw where that painting was—it's in a very remote part of the Met. People don't just stumble across that painting. How did you come across it? For that matter, what led you down this particular street? How did it happen that as you were walking down this particular street, you happened to bump into one of the few people in New York City who could explain this painting to you? Someone who learned about it only two weeks ago? What's going on here?"

Silence. A long silence. Rich's eyes are filling with tears.

"Rich, what's wrong?"

At last he speaks. "I'm dying. I have three forms of cancer."

Red alert! Red alert! The missionary looks skyward, thinking, "Lord, are You kidding me? Why me? How am I supposed to do this? We might be on the edge of eternity here!"

But he doesn't say any of that to Rich. Instead, he asks him, "Rich, do you know what hell is?"

"No."

"It's whatever you make it to be, whatever you want—but forever. So for you, it's a life without God, for eternity. That's what you've been making for yourself, and now you're close to getting it."

Gulp.

"Rich, there are too many coincidences here. Don't you see what's going on? He's throwing you a life preserver. Grab it! Come back now. There's still time."

"There's no time, either now or later. I've already missed my flight, but if I hurry, I can still catch the next one."

The missionary is on his knees out on Prince and Mulberry.

"Rich, please! This is not just you we're talking about here! I'm involved in this story, too! He sent you out here to me! I can't fail on this one! Rich, please, I'm begging you, just come into the church. Even if you don't receive reconciliation, at least come in to pray. He's trying to speak to you. Open your ears! Open your heart!"

They went on like this for another twenty minutes. Bob was beginning to wonder whether his fellow missionary would ever get back to his corner post. But the missionary was so blown away by all the crazy coincidences that had happened, he couldn't let go.

Eventually, after nearly an hour, Rich's heart and the missionary's both burning, Rich marched into the church to pray.

What happened next, the missionary doesn't know.

Rich said he was dying.

The missionary prays now, and will do so every day of his life, that Rich is living in Christ.

∞

"I don't need organized religion. I have my own relationship with God."

We hear that often. Sometimes we get a less prideful version of it: "I'm a good Catholic, but I don't go to confession. I confess my sins to God directly."

Often, people who have their "own relationship with God" are the ones who have done something they think is too embarrassing to tell a priest. We must recognize that and use some of the strategies we use for the ones who are not ready for confession (chapter 6) or who have some sin they think is unforgivable (chapter 7). But it's a very common idea in our individualistic society, where "spiritual but not religious" is a more and more common self-description.

So, how do we respond?

If someone says, "I have my own relationship with God," a question that's simple but often deeply penetrating is: "How's that working for you?" Often the answer that comes back is "Not great." That can lead to deeper dialogue.

Another good question, especially for the self-confessors, is: "How do you know He forgives you?" Also, "How do you know you're not rationalizing some bad behavior here and telling yourself He forgives you?" If a discussion ensues, remind the person that Jesus became a man, so He understands our psychology and our tendency to rationalize away bad behavior. That's why He instituted the sacrament of confession.

Another objection I file under "I have my own relationship with God" is the corollary, "I don't have any sins to confess." Usually this state of self-satisfaction is reached only by souls who have not been to confession in years and have gone on for so long rationalizing away so many bad habits that they've begun to believe — at least on the surface — that they're "good people" and that this is enough. For these people, the story of another very good person, St. Jerome — "I want your sins" (chapter 6) — is useful.

Jesus gave us the Church for a reason. Given the human condition and our tendency to rationalize, to avoid sacrifice, and to take the easy route when it's available to us, it's hard for most of us to maintain a healthy relationship with God on His terms. A few probing questions can often spark a soul to this understanding.

∞

St. Patrick's Old Cathedral, SoHo
—Spy Wednesday 2018

The back-of-the-church crew is busy all night with a steady stream of visitors being driven in by the brothers out in the byways. Jordan tells one of the missionaries he doesn't need confession. "I confess to God directly. I don't need a priest."

"Wow! That's terrific. Sometimes I feel that way too. But you know, I have two reasons why I like to go to confession."

"What are they?"

"Well, for one, it gives me great comfort to hear the voice of God, through the priest, telling me I'm forgiven. Without that, I think I would doubt that I was forgiven. The second reason—"

"Forget the second reason! The first is good enough. Which priest can I go to?"

∽

Prince and Mott, SoHo
— Holy Saturday 2017

Around 5:00, Allen returns to the corner to speak with us, now with his wife, Elizabeth, who speaks a hard-to-understand Creole dialect and little else.

Bob had spent thirty minutes with Allen yesterday, and then Cathy spent thirty more minutes with him. Allen agreed to "think about it" and come back with his wife. He was particularly impressed that Cathy had given him a prayer image of a Haitian saint, not knowing that he was Haitian.

"Wow!" he said. "That's a little weird! What moved you to give me that particular print?"

"I don't know," Cathy answered. "Maybe it was the Holy Spirit."

Now he's back for round two. Bob introduces Allen to the other missionary on the corner.

"No, we don't want to go to confession," Allen says. "We've never been. Don't need to. We talk to God on our own. But we love you guys just the same!"

The missionary goes into his pitch. Psalm 139. "Last Chance Saturday." "Time to get a big hug from Jesus." "Nothing like it!" "Special missionary priests." "Everyone who comes back is glowing." "You're named for the cousin of Mary, for goodness' sake!"

As he's selling, Elizabeth keeps pointing for more rosaries (for her daughter), more pope cards (for her niece), more Immaculate Mary medals (for her and Allen).

Finally, the missionary gets tough—well, a little tough. "Okay, that's it. You two have now taken from us approximately twelve rosaries, seven pope cards, a print of a famous Haitian saint, and four Immaculate Mary medals! That's it! You're going into that church, and you are going to confession. No more ifs, ands, or buts! Bob here will take you in."

In they march. Bob hands them over to the missionary in back. Once they're inside, they agree to pray only. Finally, the missionary in the back melts them with St. Jerome: "'I've given you the best forty years of my life, Lord! What else do you want from me?' 'Give me your sins, Jerome! Give me your sins!'"

Allen sees Fr. Stephen first. Then, given a special exception we've been allowed once before, Allen attends his wife's confession to translate from Creole to English.

Later, they appear again at Prince and Mott, all smiles, and hug us. Before heading off jubilantly, they pause for a photo.

∽

Crosby and Prince, SoHo
—Reconciliation Monday, Advent 2017

We've sent fifty seminarians out to the byways of the parish. Br. Felipe's crew is stationed here deep in SoHo. Lots of last-minute Christmas shoppers are scurrying about. Would any stop to talk?

Out of the corner of his eye, Br. Felipe notices a young man on a phone, heading west toward Tribeca, away from the parish. But the young man stops and now seems to be loitering nearby as the seminarians attempt to engage the passing crowds, flowing by at over thirty people a minute.

Br. Felipe resolves to try to engage him. As traffic temporarily dies down, he approaches with a rosary, but then—inexplicably—the rosary drops from his hand.

Seth, the young man, picks it up and offers it back to Br. Felipe.

"No, you keep it," Felipe says. "It's a gift. Are you Catholic?"

"Well, sort of. I was born Catholic."

"Do you pray much?"

"Yeah, I pray every morning, more or less. I don't go to church anymore. I have my own relationship with God."

"Wow! Awesome! What do you pray for?"

"I pray for forgiveness, mostly. Stuff I've done that I regret."

"Do you ever feel like your sin is still there, that it's not forgiven?"

"How did you know that?"

"Seth, I'm going to be a priest. It's a long road, but I'm going to make it there. And you know what drives me?"

"What, brother?"

"Mercy. I've felt it and experienced it in a very real way in the sacrament of reconciliation. Through the priest, I've felt the Lord's love. That's what drives me now. That's why I'm out here in SoHo."

"Wow! Give me some of that!"

A deeper conversation ensues, an encounter. Seth is interested. He doesn't feel ready for confession, but he's willing to head to the church and light a candle. "Brother, I'm going to go and light a candle. Something about this night is telling me to do that."

With that, Seth heads off, away from Tribeca and toward Prince and Mott and the basilica, candle in hand and love in his heart.

∞

Of course, not everyone who's not Catholic is "not religious." Many are very religious but belong to other faiths. There are our sisters and brothers from other Christian groups, of course. And in any big city you'll find many other faiths — Hindus, Jews, Buddhists, Muslims, Rastafarians.

Do we just ignore them?

Or do we try to bring Christ's love to them too?

I'll bet you know the answer already.

10

Reaching Out to Other Faiths

Prince and Mott, SoHo
—Tuesday of Holy Week 2017

It's a beautiful, joyful evening in SoHo. It appears summer has come two months early. The afternoon sun is shining warmly in our faces, and joy is in the air.

Then Khalid, a Muslim from Morocco, walks by.

"You Christians all want to kill us!" he tells one of our missionaries.

A long, initially heated discussion begins. We have lots in common. Abraham, the father of both faiths. God, who inspired Muhammad, is the same God we worship. Jesus is at least a great prophet in a Muslim context.

"But the world is going to hell! Too many of you are trying to get us!" He uses much more colorful language, but I'm not going to repeat it.

"Khalid, can you stop using those kinds of words out here on the street? You're bigger than this. You're a child of God. Come on!"

Khalid is still hostile; and the language is no less colorful. "Khalid, you're trying to rile me up, but it's not going to work. I love you too much. You're my brother. Love will always conquer hate."

"No way!"

"Khalid, I want you to go into the church to light a candle before God, and to pray for me. Can you do this for me?"

It takes some talking and a lot of Christian love, but somehow, some way (the Holy Spirit, perhaps?), Khalid finds the strength to head into a church for the first time in his life.

∽

Meanwhile, Coachella, a Catholic from Eastern Europe, chases down her friends Amanda and Amir, who have hurried off farther down Prince. Amanda is Jewish; Amir is Muslim.

"Amanda! Amir! Come on! Let's all go in together and light a candle! This is the real St. Patrick's! The original cathedral!"

Just as they're thinking about it, Khalid comes by again. "I did it!" he tells our missionary. "I lit the candle for you. I prayed for you guys!"

"Thank you, brother," says the missionary. "I love you."

Amanda and Amir do an about-face and go into the church with their friend Coachella.

∽

Our missions have been mostly about bringing in Catholics for confession, reconnecting them to the Church. But we meet all kinds of people along the way. In any big city in America, most of the people you meet won't be Catholic. You'll meet Protestants, Jehovah's Witnesses, Jews, Muslims, Buddhists, Hindus, and every other kind of religion.

We're not targeting them. But meeting them is an opportunity.

It's a chance for them to see Christ's love in action. They might even come away with a more realistic idea of what a Catholic is like.

It's also an opportunity for us, the missionaries. It's a chance to see things the way others see them. It's a chance to exercise the love Christ commanded us to show to everyone — even people who are quite different from us. This is today's version of the parable of the Good Samaritan (Luke 10:25–37).

And who knows? You may start a ball rolling. You may plant a seed. We're really all sons and daughters of God, made to be part of the communion of saints. It's just that some of us don't know it yet.

∽

Prince and Mott, SoHo
— Holy Saturday 2013

One of our missionaries spends forty-five minutes in deep conversation with Armando, a Methodist. Armando is intrigued by what he's hearing about the great history of our Faith, its integrity, its wholeness and richness distilled through two thousand years of prayer and discernment. After a long discussion, a second missionary joins the group. Then comes an unrelated newly converted Catholic man, formerly a Jew.

Finally, Armando is dragged away from this very ecumenical discussion into the surrounding din by his increasingly impatient wife. But clearly, he's thinking some thoughts he hadn't thought before. He's considering what it would mean to come back to the Catholic Faith.

∽

St. Patrick's Old Cathedral, SoHo
— Spy Wednesday 2018

Mary finds a Muslim woman in the back of the church with a candle given to her by one of the street missionaries.

"Here," the woman says." I can't light this. I'm a Muslim."

"Of course you can light it. We'd be delighted to have you light a candle for us. This is a house of God. You can light a candle and give a prayer intention."

The woman lights her candle and kneels near the front of the church to pray.

As she's leaving, she finds Mary, an Ave Maria University student helping the back-of-the-church crew. Well-formed in the faith, confident, joyful, and loving, Mary is a natural back there.

"Thank you. This is a beautiful place. You seem so young and so in love with God. Thank you for welcoming me here."

∞

Welcoming is the key. When we create an atmosphere of welcome, we show others the welcoming face of Christ. It will surprise them. If they thought of the Catholic Church as an exclusive club, they may be shocked to discover that the Church has room for them—even if they're not Catholic.

To make people feel welcome, the missionaries should have a firm idea of what the ground rules are. There aren't many. Only Catholics can receive Communion at Mass—but anyone else is welcome to come to Mass and participate in the rest of the liturgy. Only Catholics can receive the sacrament of reconciliation—but priests can talk at a spiritual level with anyone. Anyone can come in and pray. Anyone can light a candle for a prayer intention.

Once the missionaries understand that everyone is welcome, they feel comfortable welcoming everyone. And that easy welcome makes itself felt in the street.

Even the people who don't come into the church can feel the Christian love. And it makes an impression on them.

∞

Prince and Mott, SoHo
—Good Friday 2010

Near the end of the day, one of our missionaries notices an old man, South Asian, who has been observing us for some time.

Finally, the man approaches our missionary.

"Although I'm a Hindu," he says, "I support what you're doing. I can see the genuine love and joy you have for the strangers you meet, and they can, too. You obviously love every person you meet. You are making the world a better place."

∞

Most of the people of other faiths we meet are people of goodwill who respond to our goodwill. But we also meet some people who have a deep-set hostility to the Catholic Church. There's one faith that's almost always hostile, and it seems to be growing faster than any of the others.

11

Atheists and Other Hostiles

St. Patrick's Old Cathedral, SoHo
—Spy Wednesday 2014

The atheists are fired up tonight, showing up everywhere. Two of them make it all the way into the church. There, they encounter the missionary in the back of the church.

The first atheist is a middle-aged woman who says, "I'm only here to see the renovated windows." She lasts only a minute. She comes back out, gasping for air. "I can't breathe in there! Something is wrong!" (The church doors have been open wide all night, and most of us, if anything, are a little chilly.)

The second woman proclaims, "My sole interest is the architecture. Can I walk around and take pictures?"

"Of course," says our missionary. "Everyone is welcome here."

Soon, she declares proudly, "I am a devout atheist." Clenching her fist, she underscores her point. "Yes, in fact, a hard-core atheist! I don't believe any of this!"

"Wow! You seem pretty fired up."

"You should stop deceiving people! Atheism is what we should be teaching everyone!"

An atheist interested in church architecture. Hmmm. The missionary goes right past her declaration, to find out what she's really hiding underneath all those layers she's wearing. "Are you Catholic, by any chance?"

"I was baptized Catholic. But not anymore! Not since I was maybe seven years old."

The woman moves closer.

"There is no God!"

Silence.

"There are many things I do not agree with among the teachings of the Catholic Church. For one, I'm a firm believer and staunch supporter of women's reproductive rights."

"Oh, you mean you support abortion?"

"Yes, although I believe we are in agreement when it comes to supporting the poor," she says, somewhat proudly. And then she adds, "After all, you can be any religion and be a supporter of the poor."

"That is so true! In fact, we Christians support the poorest of the poor, the unborn child."

"No! No!" she protests loudly. "That is what we call 'subject to debate.'"

"Is it? Is the defenseless, weak, helpless child in the womb not poor? Especially those under threat of death?"

She retreats to lower ground. "The problem with you Catholics is that you cannot accept the reality that there is no God."

Smiling gently at her, the missionary begins naming the realities that speak strongly of the presence of God: the sun and the stars; the beauty of life; the imprint of God in our hearts; the conscience we all have in common, even when we're of different faiths; our concern for the poor and the disadvantaged; even the uplifting architecture of the church she came inside to admire.

Suddenly, the atheist declares an end to the dialogue. She has had enough. She sounds the retreat. "I need to be somewhere."

Msgr. Sakano with a missionary on Prince and Mott

Evelyn, "the missionary in the back of the church"

A missionary hailing a passerby

A missionary family in Little Italy

A missionary braving the weather

One Body in Christ

A Regnum Christi mother and her kids out on the street

A missionary dog-sitting for a penitent

The brothers with "the pope"

A missionary speaking to a group of passersby

St. Patrick's Old Cathedral, SoHo

A brother and one of our teen platoons heading out to their station

Fr. Donal at the threshold

A group of Tri-State teens pouring out of mission headquarters

Mary the missionary

The prayer team at work

As she walks somewhat hesitatingly out of the church, the missionary wonders if she isn't lighter by one layer now. Perhaps she is chewing on the same enigma the missionary is pondering. "If there is no God, why all these passionate protests against someone who doesn't exist?"

∞

Atheism is probably the fastest-growing "religion" in American cities today. When we started our street missions in New York some years ago, atheists were out and about, for sure. But few openly identified themselves as such. They just politely ignored us, or perhaps impolitely called us and the pope "pedophiles."

Now they often counter the question "Are you Catholic?" with "No way! I'm a devout atheist, and proud of it!" Often, they'll stop to engage us, to counter-evangelize us, if you will.

What do we say when the atheist comes along?

My first advice is to recognize that logic alone will not win this battle. Atheism itself requires a leap of faith. The atheist essentially believes that life was created out of thin air! That's at least as big a leap as believing that a greater being created it. You can try to point this out through a series of questions such as "How did you get here?" and "Where did the big bang itself come from?" and (for that matter) "Why do most people believe that murder is wrong? Where did we get our conscience from?"

But recognize that you're dealing with committed *believers* who are unlikely to be shaken by the facts or lack thereof.

Another approach is just to help them see the common ground they have with us. Most love life. Most believe in doing good things for their fellow man. If you can simply have a reasonably pleasant, even joyful encounter with them, you're not likely to win the day, but you may very well remove a layer of the armor that they've built up around the supposition that all religious people are intolerant fanatics incapable of relating to today's world. Gradually, this can soften them.

A third approach is to smile back at them and assure them that you and God still love them and that you will pray for them. This may be a quicker way to get to the same place. At least it will leave them thinking a bit about the encounter. And it will spare you valuable time for the next soul, who may be more fertile ground. When an atheist is engaging me, especially an unshakable one, I often wonder whether this conversation might be distracting me just as that soul Christ sent here is passing by. In these cases, I recommend cutting your losses as joyfully and pleasantly as possible and getting back to work.

∽

Lafayette and Bleecker, SoHo
—Holy Thursday 2018

Patrick's team is having a tough time. Lots of traffic, but not much interest. Across Lafayette, he sees two of his new missionaries engaged with a middle-aged woman who appears to be berating them. He crosses the street to help—remembering to approach the group with joy and love in his heart.

Giselda is telling the boys that they're wasting their time. "You guys shouldn't be out here bothering people. We're busy."

Patrick listens to her with a big winsome smile on his face. "You know, Giselda, I'm not judging you. It sounds like you don't believe in God, but we do. We've found God in the way that Jesus gave us, through his priests and the sacraments. That's what Holy Thursday is all about."

Giselda softens a little. "Well, I can't fault you guys for that. You seem like great kids."

Patrick continues: "I went to confession myself last night. First time in a year. I really feel great. Confession is a beautiful sacrament. You feel the love and mercy of God very directly. He's very real to me right now."

Now Giselda starts to open up. Turns out she's not an atheist at all. "I have to tell you guys, I do believe in God. I read the Bible a lot. I just don't buy into organized religion."

"Well, Giselda, that's a start."

They continue to talk.

Later, as Giselda is leaving the little group, she gives each of them a big hug. "I think I was meant to meet up with you guys. I really do. Somehow I feel better."

Transformed. From hater to lover.

Later, Patrick explains his success to the other missionaries. "I was in a different zone. I just went to confession myself last night, and I was in a very good place. Somehow, I just felt the love of Jesus would be the way to win this battle."

∞

Prince and Mott, SoHo
—Holy Thursday 2013

A while ago, around 3:00, busloads of joyful teens arrived, with consecrated women,[4] brothers, Regnum Christi members, and assorted lay missionaries in tow. We're certain this is a record

---

[4] The Consecrated Women of Regnum Christi are a Society of Apostolic Life and branch of the Regnum Christi Movement made up of lay women who dedicate themselves full-time to the apostolate. They live a consecrated life in the Church within the lay state.

for the number of missionaries on the street at one time—well over a hundred. It's utterly impossible for anyone with a remote interest in their spirituality to miss the chance to speak with a missionary, and eventually a priest. We have five of them waiting in the church.

The neighborhood is clearly rooting for us. Our teens keep hearing strangers call out encouragement: "Way to go!" "Your courage is inspiring!"

It seems that the nonbelievers are on their back feet. And some of them are snapping. We recognize the same angry atheist who once called me a pedophile for being a Catholic. She looks to be in as bad a mood as ever. When one of our missionaries offers her a rosary to pray on, she responds by handing the woman a bag of her dog's dung. But she leaves completely flummoxed when we respond with a loving laugh instead of the fight she was expecting.

∞

Prince and Mott, SoHo
—Good Friday 2011

About midday, a young, bearded man, identifying himself as Jewish, stops to talk to one of our missionaries, wondering why we're looking only for Catholics. "That's the problem with you people! You think you have all the answers!"

That's the beginning of a long discussion. It turns out that the young man has really cut himself off from his Jewish faith. He's drifting aimlessly toward atheism. And as energetically as he attempts to argue his positions, he seems sad.

At last, the missionary must ask: "What's wrong, Josh?"

"I feel like I have a hole in my heart."

Twenty minutes of reflective discussion follow. Finally, Josh promises the missionary to head back to the Jewish temple and renew his relationship with God.

"I will pray for you guys," Josh says. "I promise."

∽

Bleecker Street, SoHo
—Holy Saturday 2016

Br. Hunter's team out here meets a self-professed "Satanist and earth lover." Initially she's confrontational. But the brothers keep praying for her. They show her love, not hate.

"You can't have a relationship with a rock," one of them tells her. "But you can with Jesus!"

Eventually she calms down. Now she's asking them if she can confess to them right there on the street.

They encourage her to see one of our priests instead.

She won't take them up on their offer, but she seems to leave the encounter with a lighter heart.

It's important not to bring our preconceived notions to people's beliefs. To us, Satan is the name of the evil one, the adversary. But there are people who think of themselves as modern pagans, nature worshippers, and they call the principle they worship "Satan."

They're misinformed, but they're not lovers of evil. And the way we approach them is by recognizing that they want the same things we want—a world where people are good and respect God's creation. We can have a joyful encounter with them if we avoid getting hung up on a name.

Above all, we must keep showing them love. They probably call themselves Satanists because they think Christians are hateful bigots. We can surprise them.

∞

SoHo
—Holy Thursday 2015

We've got more than eighty agents of the Kingdom all over the neighborhood, spreading joy, spreading the Word, spreading love. Our teams of vibrant young people and Regnum Christi adults, consecrated women, and priests rushed out of mission headquarters at about four in the afternoon to points north, south, east, and west.

Many of the spots we've sent them to are what we call tough neighborhoods, where the world is so secular that it strikes people as almost crazy to ask, "Are you Catholic?" or "Would you like a rosary?" Yet, with joy in their hearts, they press on.

Our team in the SoHo shopping district encounters a tall man who claims to be a nonbeliever because "it's just too crazy that God would come down to earth and endure all that suffering stuff on the Cross." He seems stumped when one of our youth tells him, "Well, that's the whole point! You've got it!"

There's plenty of rejection out there, giving all of us a small sense of the mockery that Jesus endured in His Passion. We ask one atheist, "Are you Catholic?" He responds with the stupefyingly self-contradictory exclamation, "God, no!" Our teens simply love him back.

Down in Little Italy, another group asks a woman if she'd like to come to the church. But she scurries away into the busy crowd, simply telling us, "I'm afraid of God." We hope the seed of the Holy Spirit that our youth planted will gradually help her understand that God loves her and wants her back.

And despite the rejections, sometimes the power of the teens' witness stirs souls in ways unexpected. One of our teams got instant feedback from a passerby who saw how they were dealing with a grumpy homeless man near them. "Wow! You kids were so loving to that man even though he was so miserable to you! Inspirational!"

And that's the thing we must remember when we don't see success right away. Being an agent of the Kingdom is different from being the King of the Kingdom. Agents do the will of the King and don't always know how the whole plan fits together or how the story ends. Our role is to witness to His love and mercy and let Him do the rest.

Above all, never assume that a soul is out of reach just because that person doesn't look like a good prospect. Only God knows what's going on inside that person's heart. It has taken us years, but we've finally learned never to judge hastily.

12

Never Judge a Book by Its Cover

*In front of Old St. Pat's, SoHo
—Monday of Holy Week 2011*

When a young man in his late twenties strolls by with a shaved head, several body piercings, and flashy tinted glasses, Bob offers him a rosary—and is stunned when he takes it. Bob is even more surprised when he asks for a second.

While Bob is untangling the rosaries, the young man asks, "What's confession?"

Bob and the young man with the shaved head and body piercings enter into an animated discussion about the sacrament of confession, the grace it gives, and the opportunity to experience the Lord's mercy in this very direct and intimate way. Right there on Prince and Mott.

Bob's goal here is just to get this guy into the church. He's hoping his missionary colleagues in the back of the church will take him from there. Eventually he succeeds. Then they do.

Sometime later, the young man emerges, glowing. He's not asking, "What's confession?" anymore. He has experienced it firsthand.

∞

One of my father's favorite warnings when I was growing up was "Don't judge a book by its cover. Better yet, don't judge. Love."

I never really understood how much cover judging I tended to do until we started our Holy Week missions in New York.

On the one hand, cases that would seem to be layups — well-dressed, holy-looking souls seemingly headed toward the church — often proved to be the most difficult to get to confession. "I know Msgr. Sakano" seemed to be their favorite defense. Our typical response — "And?" — would often, but not always, lead to a discussion about the sacrament of reconciliation and an eventual deeper conversion. But few of these holy-looking ones were easy targets.

On the other hand — especially in the early years of the mission — I tended to ignore people who seemed too far gone, too offbeat, too sloppily clothed, or just too different. That proved to be very poor judgment indeed. Often our deepest encounters have been with people we least suspected of having an interest in coming to church: indigent-looking street-walkers; young men or women with multiple body piercings; food-delivery bikers; same-sex couples walking hand in hand; self-identified Jewish, Muslim, or Buddhist followers; an ex-con packing heat; even a scantily clad young woman on her way to perform at a strip club.

Today, we almost always seek these folks out. Having been knocked over the head time and again by the Holy Spirit, we've finally arrived at our St. Paul moment. We realize now at an instinctive level that we are all truly "one body in Christ."

Understanding at this very deep level that everyone we meet on the streets is indeed made in the image of God — and therefore has special dignity as a soul who will live forever—is a game-changer. Once you truly understand and believe that each person you encounter is a child of God, your attitude toward that soul is perceptibly altered.

I'm convinced that one reason for our success over the years has been that each soul we encounter on the streets can feel the respect with which we approach them, and that attracts them to us. In the process, they find new respect for themselves. As they discover that, they find a bigger reason to come back to their Creator.

∞

Prince and Mott, SoHo
—Tuesday of Holy Week 2017

Bob is talking with a young man named—I'm not kidding—Jesus. He has a T-shirt on that says, "Kill them all."

"You know, Jesus, even though you don't think you're Catholic, you are. Once you're baptized Catholic, you're forever Catholic, a child of God. And He is seeking you always. Come back. Ask for His forgiveness."

Jesus is deep in thought, engaged.

At that moment, Tiffany and Waddell stop by. Half an hour before, Bob had sent them into the church for a "quick visit." Now it's half an hour later, and they're both smiling.

"Thank you for asking us in," says Tiffany. "It was beautiful."

Jesus takes a rosary and promises to come back for confession later this week.

Jake, a young man with long hair and large bright-blue eyeglasses (the kind of "unlikely" Catholic we've learned not to overlook) stops when asked if he's Catholic. His friend Luca keeps moving. Luca is "not Catholic," but Jake is.

"Hold on a minute here," says Jake. "I'm Catholic, and I'd like a rosary, please."

"Luca, are you really not Catholic?" asks Bob.

"Well, my mother was."

"We have a lot of that going on tonight, Luca. And here's the good news — you *are* Catholic if you were baptized Catholic!"

"Wow! Then I am Catholic after all!"

They both head in to pray.

∞

Of all the unlikely prospects out there, "alternative lifestyles" may be the hardest for new missionaries to deal with.

It is not a well-guarded secret that one of the greatest obstacles between today's secularized Catholics and the Church is sexual morality. For us missionaries on the streets, issues surrounding sexual morality are often present, the subtext of whatever discussion we may be having with a passerby.

So, it's important to have something to say about it.

In SoHo, a hotbed of alternative lifestyles, it's not uncommon to receive somewhat awkward laughs or giggles from a passing same-sex couple walking together, even as one admits he or she "was once a Catholic." Some will even stop to talk.

If there's one thought to convey in this situation, it's that the Church doesn't condemn gay people. The missionary needs to convey that. Quite the opposite, in fact: we're open to all, we love all — including those attracted to the same sex. For many, this will be a big surprise, and getting them into the church to pray will be a good start.

Further, only God gets to judge us. So frankly, it's not up to the missionaries to do any excluding. This openness to others is true for sure at the office, and it is also true on the streets. As missionaries on the streets, our goal is to bring everyone to God, through the mechanism of the Church, and let Him handle the rest. It is not for us to judge.

If you've taken the conversation this far, you can encourage the people you've met to talk to one of your priests. The priest may or may not be able to give them absolution. But he might bring them closer to an understanding of what God wants for them.

Another stumbling block can be young couples living together whose union is not recognized by the Church. Again, we usually don't take it upon ourselves to preach doctrine on the streets. Rather, we welcome people with open arms and invite them into the church for prayer and confession. We realize that all these young people — gay, heterosexual, or something in between — are on a journey, and it's important at least to help them get the graces they can to keep moving in the right direction. The Lord in His good time will help them come to a deeper understanding of the importance of His sacraments, especially marriage.

In some ways, the more difficult souls to get back into the church are not the ones blissfully ignorant of the Church's moral teaching on marriage, but rather, the ones who understand it yet don't feel that they can do anything about it. For example, at least once a year, I catch up with a hard-working immigrant in the neighborhood who delivers meals from the local eateries to the many apartment dwellers of NoLIta. Temporarily separated from his family in Costa Rica, he hints that he's settled in with a girlfriend here in New York. Brought up in the Faith in a conservative culture, he knows that what he's doing is against Church teaching, but he feels, perhaps out of loneliness, that he has no alternative. Every year, I receive from him a different reason for not cleaning this up by talking to our priests. "I'm working." "I know I need to go, and I'll come back later." Still, I persist lovingly. I know the Holy Spirit is working here in deeper ways. "All in God's good time."

Another similar obstacle of passion these days is pornography addiction. Statistics tell us that a good percentage of the men, and some of the women we encounter are struggling with this problem. They know intuitively that this habit is not approved of by the Church, or even perhaps by themselves. They suspect that it is not good for their souls. Most won't want to speak about it directly, although some will refer to a habit "that I know I need to give up, but I really don't want to right now."

Again, it's very difficult in a single street encounter to bring someone to a resolution to address this habit. But you can gently encourage them to get the help from God that they need and—deep down—want.

"John, look, you're doing something you believe is wrong, but you can't give it up right now. I get that. But how do you feel about this?"

"Not great" is the usual answer.

"Well, that's a start: that's a sign of contrition of sorts. Why not bring that to God through the priests? Maybe He can help you through this—give you the graces you need to get to a better place."

A similar angle would be, "John, look, we're all on a journey here. None of us are perfect. We've all done some pretty bad things. Being perfect is not the important thing; staying on a path to be better is. Come into the church and pray on this at least. God wants you back. He wants what's good for you."

In many of our encounters, we sense that a sin of passion is at the center of the problem, but the person doesn't usually tell us what it is.

One thing is certain. When a sin of passion is involved, the glow of a soul suddenly finding himself forgiven when he had least expected it is very bright indeed.

Sometimes—in fact, most of the time—you won't get to see that glow. You'll know only that you talked with someone for a while—someone who seemed to be interested but went away without making a commitment.

Just remember that your efforts aren't wasted. It may help to think of yourself as a sower.

13

Sowing Seeds

SoHo
—Saturday of the Third Week of Advent 2011

Today's mission has been long and difficult, beginning with a procession to the abortion clinic, enduring the hecklers there, and then a long afternoon in SoHo among the busy Christmas shoppers.

We've got a dozen missionaries at work. We estimate that we've greeted some 10,000 souls, engaged 250 for sidewalk talks, and brought 100 to church and 50 to confession, most of those the first in a long time. Daunting numbers!

Over and over we called, "Are you Catholic?" Over and over the response came back, "No." It became almost like a meditation, with a rhythmic cadence—interrupted perhaps one time in thirty by a short dialogue with someone searching for the Faith. It became our prayer.

And, incredibly, despite the long odds against success—and some days even worse—we could feel the Lord beside us, energizing us and making us joyful and happy. We could sense ourselves planting seeds.

Jesus' parable of the sower appears in three of the Gospels (Matt. 13:3–9; Mark 4:3–9; Luke 8:4–8). The sower plants seeds everywhere, but not all the seeds grow into useful grain—only the ones that fall in good soil.

And here's the thing: even when we plant a seed in good soil, we don't get a harvest right away.

We must be patient.

We must have faith.

Many of the seeds we've sown today fell on hard ground.

Many others are still germinating, and we may never know what became of them: the deliveryman Miguel who was hurrying off to work but was visibly touched and promised to go to confession before Christmas; the young man who asked for rosaries for himself and the friends he was on his way to visit; the young mother who asked about religious education for her child just as the person who could answer that question, Msgr. Sakano, arrived at the corner to buck us up; the thirty-something, fashionably dressed woman we met who fondly recalled to us a Regnum Christi mission she had been on in her home country of Mexico, then hurried on her way to shopping in SoHo without stopping at the church; the Jesuit priest, dressed in civilian clothes and out shopping himself, who seemed moved by the mission and then blessed us there on the street corner before he hurried off.

Today, some seeds bore immediate fruit. One group of middle-aged women were sent into the Church for a prayer, and they emerged all smiles and joy nearly an hour later, after receiving reconciliation.

One of our most successful missionaries today was a man we had encountered the year before who returned to help us this year; he worked with us all day yesterday and today, and touched many. Another person we met last April came rushing toward us late in the day, asking if there was still time to receive reconciliation. There was, and she did. A third, now an active member of the parish, met us for the reception after Mass and joyfully recalled his chat two years ago on the street corner with one of our missionaries.

As missionaries, too often we want to see what happens, to know the ending. It's a natural part of our human nature. But that's not our role. We're part of a bigger scheme, a larger picture. We're workers in the vineyard. Sowers of the seed.

∞

When we're out on the streets, it's easy to feel as though we're wasting our time. We greet 10,000 to get 50 to confession. What about the other 9,950 we greeted, or at least the other 200 whom we managed to get into a dialogue with? And even the 50 whom we brought to confession—will they take the grace they were given in the sacrament and put it to use in building up their lives?

It's frustrating not to know. We do all that hard work on the streets and in the church. We want to see results now.

But, like good farmers, we must be patient. We must plant the seeds and wait for them to grow in God's own time.

∞

Prince and Mott, SoHo
—Good Friday 2015

A middle-aged couple passes us on their way to dinner.

They are happy to stop for a chat. The man is just back from "twenty years away" and has met the woman recently. He found his faith somewhere in the depths of prison and got his girlfriend to start going to Mass after many years away.

"Confession?" he asks. "You're kidding!"

We talk for a long time about the grace of this sacrament and the transformative power of grace.

The girlfriend becomes more agitated, nervous. She's starting to chain-smoke.

The discussion moves on, probing deeper.

Finally, the missionary and the boyfriend escort the woman, now almost in tears, to the sacrament.

Later, the ex-con turns to the missionary. "You know what got her? You kept talking about grace."

"Yes, grace is what it's all about!"

"No, you don't get it. Her middle name is Grace."

∞

Broadway and Lafayette, SoHo
—Holy Thursday 2017

Patrick, one of our enthusiastic veterans from previous missions, is out here with the pope cutout. He and his team are offering selfies with the pope and hoping that leads deeper.

It often does.

Bill walks over.

"Are you Catholic?" Patrick asks.

"No, and I'm not interested. Thank you, though." He hurries off.

A minute later, he returns to the pope. "What's the deal with you guys? What are you doing this for?"

"We came from all over the Tri-State area to help people find their way back to God. This is our little mission for Jesus during Holy Week."

"Really? That's crazy. You're wasting your time here, guys. This is New York City!"

"We don't think we're wasting our time. We've met a lot of people, and many of them have gone to visit the church. Why don't you come for a visit?"

"Are you kidding? I'm not Catholic! I don't believe!"

"Are you really not Catholic? You seem like you might be Catholic, Bill."

"Well, okay, I was baptized Catholic. My mom was Catholic, but Dad never was a believer. And I'm not either."

"Bill, is that all there is to your story? You're holding something back."

"Well, okay, I went to a Catholic college at my mother's urging. And I really loved it. I was surrounded by Catholics, and I kind of got into it then. But now I'm here, in New York City, and there are no Catholics and frankly I've lost my faith."

Wow!

"Bill, everything happens for a reason."

"I believe that, Patrick."

"We met for a reason."

"I believe that too."

"Come back, Bill. Come to confession and reconcile with Jesus."

"I can't, Patrick. I'm too far gone. I have too many sins. I can never go back now."

"Bill, the Lord will forgive you. He always forgives us. He loves us like a father, like your father, like your mother. His doors are always open for you."

With that, Bill slips off, into the city.

"But I know we removed a layer, Steve," Patrick says when he tells me this story. "I could see it happening. I could see the seed of rebirth being planted in Bill, right before my eyes; I feel like I was witnessing a miracle."

∝∞

Bleecker and Mulberry, border of Greenwich Village
— Holy Saturday 2013

Way up here at the "brothers' station," Br. Patrick meets a woman named Shakira. She was baptized a Catholic, but she has never been to confession. Like many on the streets these days, she has been trying to keep to herself, earphones on, music blaring. "Me. Me. Me."

Somehow, by means of the good brothers, the Holy Spirit has broken through to her.

Now they're walking and talking all the way back to the cathedral — the three of them: Br. Patrick, Shakira, and the Holy Spirit.

We have no idea how much this chance encounter (which I'm sure wasn't really "chance") may have changed Shakira's life. But she's one of us now, a more complete part of the body of Christ. Of "us," not just "me."

∝∞

Broome and Mott, Little Italy
— Holy Thursday 2012

One particularly "on fire" young missionary, Janet, spies a famous actress out in the streets and invites her into the church. They get into a deep discussion, and it turns out that the actress had a similar chat with some friends over dinner just the night before. She pulls out her phone, sets it to "video," and asks Janet to repeat her "pickup line" so she can play it back to her friends. We have no idea how far this particular chain will extend.

Sowing Seeds

∽

Prince and Mott, SoHo
—Monday of Holy Week 2017

A young woman approaches, decked out in very showy attire. Underneath all the makeup, her natural beauty still shines forth.

"Are you guys really Catholic? I didn't think there were any Catholics left!"

"Oh, there are quite a few of us left. It's a joyful Faith to be a part of!"

"I'm sort of Catholic. At least I was. Can I have a rosary?"

"Of course. What color?"

"I'll take purple."

"Where are you going? We have lots to talk about."

"I've got to run! I'm a stripper now. But I'm going to pray on this rosary."

From previous experience, we believe she'll be back next year.

∽

SoHo
—Friday of the Second Week of Advent 2012

A group of young women, dressed for a night on the town, initially passes us giddily, seemingly uninterested. Eventually one confesses to being Catholic and then turns in the other three. Half a block of walking and talking later, all four head into the church for confession.

The Regnum Christi Mission Corps—young men giving a pre-college year to Christ—have been out on the perimeter, and now we're seeing the souls they've sent in. Some of them had only grabbed a pamphlet and moved on. But that started something in their hearts, and once they get near the church, they turn inside.

Bob is hailing the usual bike messengers. Following his example, another missionary approaches a flower delivery man who promises to return after his shift. Seeds planted, fruits harvested.

One man, asked if he'd like a rosary, replies, "No, thank you! I'm still using the one you guys gave me last year!"

The sidewalk hat vendor we finally cracked last year looks very happy to see us now. He instantly launches into a vigorous discussion of God and religion. His cheerful wife confides, "He only talks about this stuff with you guys."

For every "I'm going in," we get three who say "I'll be back." We're praying that the Holy Spirit guides these souls home.

∞

St. Patrick's Old Cathedral, SoHo
—Wednesday of Holy Week 2012

We're hearing stories from our missionaries who were all over the neighborhood.

There's the story of Robert, who approached one of our brothers out on a street corner, crying. He had talked with our Br. Laslow during the Ash Wednesday mission and was touched by the Holy Spirit, though he didn't go to confession then. Now he wanted to take that next step and needed the brothers to bring him.

Our brothers in Little Italy fenced with a French atheist who, after an extensive dialogue, seemed shaken and then retreated, declaring a "draw."

A brother who was stationed in SoHo tells me he walked someone into confession from Lafayette Street. I promise him

I'll get out my tape measure to determine whether he's broken last night's record confession walk from Little Italy.

Our consecrated women in front of the church snagged a visitor there, found out it was her birthday, and convinced her to give Christ her confession as a birthday gift. We've had several returnees from earlier in the week—some who had gone to confession and were beaming when they met us on the street, others who had promised to come back for confession and did. We had one young woman who, after another pep talk, determined to go back to confession for a second round. In her face, which was anxious and tormented last night, we saw peace tonight.

Our missionaries in front of the church had a similar experience. A man came in with a pamphlet from the brothers out on the periphery. He got a pep talk in front of the church, went in and prayed, came back out for another pep talk, and eventually left unconfessed with the promise to return tomorrow.

So many seeds planted by the Holy Spirit tonight. We hope to reap the harvest as the Triduum begins and our young people arrive in force.

But already we see the benefits. As I'm hurrying off to Mass, one brother shouts to me, "This was the best day of my life! So many wonderful conversations with people about their Faith!"

And another simply and joyfully declares, "Christ must be so happy tonight."

∞

St. Patrick's Old Cathedral, SoHo
—Ash Wednesday 2017

In the congregation for 7:00 Mass, we spy several folks from our chats out on Prince and Mott.

Donald is one of them. He's a thirty-something man we first met three years ago. Back then, Bob and I had a long chat with him about the Faith, and about how confession is a personal gift we can give to God, a chance to return God's love for us, to let Him love us, to enter a relationship with Him. Afterward, he left us, moved on—said he wasn't ready.

"God bless you," Bob said as he moved on.

But today Donald showed up at Prince and Mott. He remembered our encounter from three years back, and he recounted the conversation in detail when one of us approached him again as he walked past.

"Is the invitation still open? Will a priest hear my confession now?"

"Of course! But this seems too easy! Didn't you say it's been many years since your last confession?"

"I did. But, you see, what you said three years ago about confession being a gift to Jesus—it's been ringing in my ears ever since. I can't get it out of my head."

∞

Prince and Mott, SoHo
—Friday of the Second Week of Advent 2015

Late in the evening, an attractively dressed woman appears on the corner and asks, "Do you remember me?"

At first, the missionary doesn't recognize her, until she says, "You promised to pray for me on a certain day."

"Of course I remember you! I prayed for you on May 22. I kept the date in my phone. You didn't tell me then what it was about or why, but I prayed for you that morning."

"Yes, May 22! Thank you. I felt you had. It went really well."

The woman had not been to confession since the day the missionary had met her nearly a year ago, but she was praying daily now, and she looked far more well-kept, more serene, and less nervous than at their last encounter. She had given up chain-smoking. She was further in her spiritual journey, and this time readily accepted the offer to pray in the church. She even received reconciliation again.

On the way in, from somewhere deep in the missionary's mind, the woman's middle name springs to his tongue.

"Your middle name is Grace."

"You're kidding! I'm that important? You remembered my middle name?"

"I didn't. He did."

And at that moment the missionary understands why the whole crew has been laboring five hours on a quiet night in SoHo. To welcome back Grace. To be there for her return.

14

Success!

SoHo
—*Good Friday 2012*

This morning, our two bands of teens carried two giant "prayer crosses" from Times Square and Central Park to St. Pat's Old Cathedral, with passersby nailing their intentions to the cross as they progressed. Our Times Square team carried a distressed woman's intention for her gravely ill father's health in this world and the next: in her words, he had "given up." The young woman ended up joining the crew, carrying the cross to us from uptown. Our teens, joined by a young member of the parish in the role of the captain of the Roman guards, beautifully and reverently reenacted the Way of the Cross through Little Italy and SoHo. Once again, they shut the place down and converted many hearts with their loving witness.

Today's 3:00 liturgy was standing room only, and the crowd, twenty people across, reverently following the Way of the Cross, snaked through the streets for a hundred yards at least.

Various new records were set for the types of vehicles flagged down for a talk about the Faith: the FedEx carrier pushing a stack of boxes through the intersection on a cart, the woman in the back of a pedicab who took a rosary, the pizza delivery bike (was it the same guy we talked to last year?), the police officer flagged in his patrol car who promised, after a long talk, to return after work for confession.

It seems like many Catholics and ex-Catholics have been feeling the tug of the Lord's love today. All we seem to be doing is giving them that extra nudge.

And little miracles abound everywhere. During the Way of the Cross, when the front of the church was temporarily unmanned, the three sisters from the white dog story and their brother Brendan unexpectedly arrived as if on cue and took over. Within minutes, Joan had a woman newly emerged from her first confession in many years, crying for joy and kissing and hugging her for being there.

Another woman literally came skipping out of the church for joy, and later another pair of young women performed this same confession dance. They said they'd gone in feeling that "something in me needed to change" and were rejoicing because "now it has."

One of our youngest missionaries, Meghan, set a record by getting a man to the church and the Way the Cross who hadn't been to church since before Meghan was born.

Running out of rosaries by midday, we fell back on Our Lady of Lourdes medals, which we began calling "confession medals," giving them to people as they streamed back from the confessionals to thank us.

One woman who was invited with two friends into confession was so tearfully moved when she emerged that she called her husband on her cell phone and asked him to come and receive the sacrament too. He did, and they left the church hand in hand, seemingly at peace.

Late in the day, Thomas walked into the church. The missionary in the back invited him to confession. Thomas emerged joyfully later and returned to kiss and hug her. Then he asked for one of her plastic rosaries. When she gave him one, he pulled from his neck his own rosary, blessed at Lourdes and Fatima, and presented it to her for healing.

That missionary in the back of the church suffers from "incurable but treatable" blood cancer. Somehow, Thomas seemed to know this. Another of those mysterious "coincidences."

∞

When we first started our missions on the streets of New York, I wasn't very optimistic, as you know. I thought there was no way it could work.

And that's probably the way every missionary feels at the beginning. All we can see is the impossible task ahead of us.

One after another, people walk by, ignoring us or insulting us. What good is this doing? Will we ever get anywhere?

But all the time we're planting seeds. And after a while, if we persist, we begin to see the harvest.

We hardly realize it at first, but those seeds are growing, slowly and steadily. After a lot of work, we come to a sudden realization: this mission is beginning to look like a success!

∞

All over town
—Holy Saturday 2014

Our missionary numbers have reached a crescendo, with up to 140 missionaries out on the streets at times during the day. Today our Good Friday team has been reinforced by the teen group from St. Peter's, and by Fr. Justin's busload of families from Cheshire.

It hasn't been all easy going. Fr. Shane's team has it particularly hard, going out into stations 25 and 26, deep in SoHo: big crowds, but so focused on shopping for shiny things of this world that they have little time for a chat about the next.

But persistence has paid off. Two Cheshire families near the abortion clinic, led by our six-year-old missionary rock star, have managed to find takers for their entire stock of pope cards. Another Cheshire team, this one in Little Italy, engaged the star of the 1980s movie *Sixteen Candles*. Through the long afternoon, our missionaries have stuck to their posts, pouring themselves out. Gradually our supply of Pope Francis cards ran out, then the rosaries, then the Lourdes medals, and even our house blessing cards.

We've seen lots of love up in Harlem at the teens' "Angel for a Day" program; on the streets of SoHo with people wearing or carrying our rosaries; and on Prince and Mott, where we've had lots of lively discussions of faith. Throughout the day, souls touched by a missionary out in the byways have somehow found their way to the church.

Once they got there, every one of them seemed to have an issue—a reason to go into the church, but also a fear of going in there. One by one, we loved them in—even the ones caught in the act of escape. A family of six emerged reconciled in midafternoon, but as we were handing out Our Lady of Lourdes "confession medals," one of the young mothers, along with the grandmother, admitted that they hadn't actually gone to confession. Back we lovingly marched them! When they emerged a second time, the whole extended family was glowing.

Love begot joy—lots of it; Br. Alonso's teen group rotated all afternoon between their assigned stations and the "hymn station" on Lafayette and Spring, serenading the neighborhood with songs of God's grace. Throughout the afternoon, joyful souls streamed from church, hugging the missionaries, with their beautiful Easter glow on.

Success!

A young man in Little Italy stopped by "Seal Team Six" for directions; they sent him to church instead. After he had prayed there, our missionary in the back invited him to his first confession in thirteen years. Since his fiancée was killed in 9/11, he had spent his days "hating God." When he emerged, reconciled, he sought out the teen who had found him lost in Little Italy. "Thank you. You changed my life. You lifted a weight. I love God again!"

And the hat seller on Prince and Mott, who, years before, had chased us off "his" corner, was so moved by all the love and joy around him that in midafternoon he showed up at the mission store with a donation of a hundred hats for our missionary teens. It was a cold night. The hats, and the love they represented, warmed us.

∽

SoHo
—Holy Thursday 2013

After a short spiritual pep talk, our teens rushed out into the streets and manned their posts joyfully all afternoon. Most of them had to be pried away when it was time to come back for a slice of pizza and, later, the Mass of the Lord's Supper.

The whole neighborhood is abuzz and gripped by the excitement. People keep coming up to the missionaries in front of the church and turning themselves in: "What's going on here?" "What's all the excitement about?" "It's inspiring to see so many Catholics standing up for the Faith!" "We didn't think Catholics did this kind of thing!"

Our Lumen band on Prince and Mott has been showing us the power of businessmen with infectious personalities when their talents are applied to the Lord's work. Many of them are here for the first time, and at first, they seem a little startled by some of the brush back pitches that get thrown at us when we ask, "Excuse me, are you Catholic?"

"Been there, done that!"

"Are you kidding?"

"No! Atheist!"

And sometimes worse.

But now they've found their groove, chasing down people "too busy" to stop and engaging them so joyfully that these people end up in the church.

In fact, they've got a competition of sorts going on. At any one time, it seems that at least two of the Prince and Mott crew are doing the confession walk with a passerby who was "too busy." One stock trader got netted when he was invited to ask investment advice from the Wall Street missionary and ended up in confession instead.

And then there's Bob's latest exploit: evangelizing a man while his target was on a cell-phone call and escorting him all the way to church while he was still conducting his phone conversation. I don't have the imagination to make this stuff up!

∞

Prince and Mott, SoHo
—Saturday of the Second Week of Advent 2012

Our little band was overjoyed by the arrival at 2:30 of Fr. Shane and his troop of teens from St. Peter's parish in Yonkers. We've divided them into six teams, and now they've encircled the parish. Through the long afternoon they've stayed at their posts, smiling joyfully and witnessing to the neighborhood that the

Lord is still with us all. There have been several encounters with atheists, who in general seem off balance in the face of our joyful youths. Some asked to take their pictures with our missionaries.

In one case, Bob and Abdul convinced a young woman named Roxanne to join them on the spot; Bob gave her a mission shirt, and she evangelized with them on the corner for over an hour. There was something about her that just projected love. She was incredibly successful in engaging people. Finally, she had to move on to whatever she had been going to do nearly two hours before.

The confession lines have been six deep at times. We've had at least two examples of people who felt the call to join the Church. One, Victoria, promised we'd see her being baptized at the Easter Vigil Mass this spring. Another, T.J., walked back to the corner from several blocks away and said, "You know, I turned down that rosary you're holding because I'm not Catholic. But I really need a community of faith. Can I have a rosary? Will you take me in?"

One of our missionaries is named Grace, and we have a story about her, too. It's evening, and two men float from the church toward Prince and Mott. The larger one wraps me in a bear hug, shouting, "I'm so happy I could scream!"

He says he'd been carrying sins around with him for twenty-five years, but now they are forgiven. "I feel like I just lost fifty pounds!"

"What happened, John?" we ask.

"That wonderful young woman you have in front of the church got me! I had no plans at all to go to confession, especially after twenty-five years. But she was so engaging, so loving, she finally talked me into it. I wish I knew her name."

"That was Grace," we reply.

"That's it!" John says. "Grace sent me! I was delivered by grace!"

THE MISSIONARY OF WALL STREET

∞

Prince and Mott, SoHo
—Holy Tuesday 2013

Yesterday we had some of the worst weather these missions have seen: cold, rain, some sleet, and wind. But after all that, today the streets of SoHo seem washed clean. A calm has come over the place.

When we started out this evening, it seemed as if most of the neighborhood's inhabitants and visitors were still hiding inside. We were expecting one of those quiet nights—and a good thing, we thought. What can our little band of four missionaries, two brothers, and two priests possibly do anyway?

Answer: not much, but that's not counting the Big Guy.

Suddenly, around 6:00, the sun came out, and the heavens opened with souls. Many of them are responding to us with smiles and joy, even if they're not the Catholics we're looking for.

Languages seem to be no barrier. The brothers with us were able to help us bring in a Spanish speaker on his way to work: we had shakily gotten him as far as the church, where they were able to reassure him in Spanish that our missionary priests could speak his language.

Somehow, Abdul has netted a Chinese-speaking man. The man is clearly Catholic, but he doesn't speak our language. That doesn't stop Abdul. He's using sign language and mime—and getting the point across. There goes the man into the church.

Two bystanders outside the cupcake shop were watching Abdul's performance. His gesticulations were so effective that now they're heading in for confession too.

Meanwhile, the Lord has been using Bob's evangelical athleticism to score two doubles—bringing two people in to reconciliation with one encounter. Well, the rest of us aren't going to let him get ahead of us.

Our missionary at the back of the church tells us about the Englishman she approached. He was clearly praying but keeping his distance. After a discussion with Fr. Jason, he's now discerning conversion. And our missionary has convinced another penitent, Bianca, to join us on the streets on Friday.

Even when we have just a few people out on the streets, the Holy Spirit can do wonderful things with us. It's partly because we've prepared, planning our mission carefully, and honing our pickup lines. It's partly because we've gotten ourselves ready: going to confession, praying, reading. But it's mostly because we trust the Holy Spirit and let Him do His work through us. That, more than anything else, is what makes a successful missionary.

∞

Prince and Mott, SoHo
—Friday of the Second Week of Advent 2013

More and more, the scene out on the street corners and in front of the church is taking on the mood of a festival. In a kind of "Little Drummer Boy" moment, an old man who works at the New Museum down the street, in gratitude for our gifts of candles, rosaries, and prayer cards, reaches into his bag for a harmonica. Quietly and joyfully, he plays for us a very special hymn: the Salve Regina.

Sr. Antoniana and Sr. Veronica from the Sisters of Life[5] are particularly unstoppable tonight. People simply melt in their

---

[5] The Sisters of Life is a religious community of women founded in 1991 by John Cardinal O'Connor for the protection and enhancement of the sacredness of every human life.

joyful hands. Their entire routine consists of inviting people on the corner to light a candle, then walking them to the church, talking joyfully along the way. By the time they get to the church, they're best friends. Many come back to the corner later to hug them as if they've known them their whole lives.

The whole movement is so natural, it seems as if they're running a kind of preplanned ushering service. Neither one has to stand on the corner for more than a minute before another soul shows up for her to escort happily to the church for a candlelight visit with our Lord.

Now it's getting close to time to go.

It's nearly 9:00.

None of the missionaries, despite being frozen to the bone, want to leave their posts. But I finally persuade them to pack up. I need to spend a moment with the Lord.

I walk into the church, and as I enter, I nearly break down in tears.

From out on the streets, I could never have imagined the scene within. As the musicians strum a joyful Spanish hymn on their guitars, nearly a hundred people are on their knees, praying with the Lord. Our five priests are all busy with penitents.

And at the center of it all, lit by the candles of those present and others who have already left with spirits renewed, is our Lord on the altar.

I think back to how quietly the evening began. I would never have expected to see this multitude of souls before God at the conclusion — I'm in awe of His power, grace, and love.

And I remember what Sr. Antoniana kept telling everyone: "All you have to do is ask."

15

The Rewards of Being a Missionary

Lafayette and Kenmare, SoHo
—Good Friday 2018

Br. Leonardo's team has been sent out to the triangular park bordering Lafayette and Kenmare. Brother deploys his team to all four corners of the intersection, each brother alone at his post. Vulnerable positioning.

A homeless man in a wheelchair approaches Br. Felipe, who's standing bravely alone at the far southern end of the triangle. "Do you have a few dollars you can give me, Father?"

"I'm sorry, I'm just a brother. But in any case, I take a vow of poverty. I don't have a dime. But I have a rosary. It's worth more. You can use it to pray to Mary."

His name is Michael, and he has a fresh gash on his forehead with a bandage over it. "I was beaten and robbed for six dollars last night. I feel so defeated." He begins to cry.

"You know, Michael, today is Good Friday. On Good Friday, we celebrate Jesus' Passion on the Cross. He suffered greatly to save us. He loves us. He loves you."

Michael is crying more now.

"Jesus loves you, Michael. You are not alone. Jesus suffered a blow like the one you have now on your forehead. But Jesus knew that His Father had not abandoned Him. And He has not abandoned you."

Michael is wiping the tears from his eyes. He and Br. Felipe hold hands silently for a moment, brothers in Christ. Then Michael begins to shake Br. Felipe's hand firmly, with deeply moving sincerity and love.

Brother pats him lovingly on the shoulder.

Michael straightens up, thanks him one more time, and wheels himself off into the bustle of Lafayette.

I've been watching this whole scene, and I couldn't resist snapping a photo from afar. Now I approach Br. Felipe.

"Brother," I say, "that was very moving. That's what this mission is all about."

"Steve, this was very deep for me. I felt what it's like to be a priest. I felt what it's like to reach out to a suffering soul in need of the love of Christ. I felt the heart of Jesus."

∞

Missions transform everyone touched by them — including the missionaries.

All of us have been deeply impacted by our participation in this special apostolate, from the youngest of us to the oldest. There's something very special about the opportunity to work hand in hand with the Holy Spirit and to witness His intervention so many times that the word "coincidence" just naturally begins to drop from our vocabulary to be replaced by "another little miracle."

Relationships are deepened through shared experience, and for many of us, this mission has been the ultimate shared experience with Christ. Every little miracle along the way deepens and enriches that relationship. Our faith is no longer an endpoint reached weekly at Sunday Mass. Now it's something more like a journey, with ups and downs, peaks and valleys, glimpses of the light and then of the darkness. Through the mission, faith becomes tangible, real. On the streets, working hand in hand with Christ, the missionaries feel His grace. They are no longer alone.

When I meet persons who worked on the mission several years ago, they sometimes excitedly blurt out how, years later, the experience is still having a profound influence on their lives. Their memory of some encounter with a soul, which might have lasted only a few minutes, but in which they saw the face of Christ, lingers clear as ever.

∞

Mulberry and Broome, Little Italy
— Reconciliation Monday, Advent 2017

Br. Peter and his crew are hailing down visitors in busy Little Italy.

Joan appears out of the darkness, wearing a white coat.

"Are you Catholic?"

"Sort of."

"Would you like a rosary? It was blessed at the basilica by Msgr. Sakano."

Joan puts out her cigarette and takes the rosary.

"When was the last time you held a rosary, Joan?"

"My mom gave me one, years ago. I lost it."

"Joan, we're here tonight to offer reconciliation. We have missionary priests up at the basilica hearing confessions. They're amazing. When was the last time you had a chance to receive reconciliation?"

"Wow! That was a long time ago." Joan replies. "I've done some things that are probably unforgivable."

"Joan, nothing is unforgivable for the Lord. He just wants you to come home. He loves you."

"I can't go. I've got to get my Christmas presents wrapped."

"Joan, really? We're talking about eternal forgiveness here! And you have to get your Christmas presents wrapped?"

"I've had a really tough year, Brother ..."

Joan breaks down in tears on the street. She's going to the church. Brother starts to walk with her, talking through her issues. Finally, she gains strength.

"Brother, thank you. I'm ready. I'm going. Now I want you to do me a big favor."

"What's that, Joan?"

"I want you to go back to that corner. You've already healed me, or at least started me on the path. I'm going in. But I don't want to be the cause of your missing another person who needs you as I did. Get back out there!"

Br. Peter heads back to Mulberry and Broome; Joan heads to St. Patrick's Old Cathedral.

Later, after Mass, Joan finds Br. Peter in the back of the church.

She has a giant, teary smile on her face. She thanks him and heads off lightly into the night.

∞

Prince and Mott, SoHo
—Holy Thursday 2017

A fashionable young woman, glowing, arrives from the church. "Can you help me find one of your missionaries? She was a beautiful teenage girl, very joyful! She saved me!"

This doesn't narrow our group down very well, but it's an opening.

"Did she get you to go to confession, Vivian?"

"Yes! Exactly! How did you know?"

"We could see the glow. We call it the 'confession afterglow.' You're shining!"

"You got it! I feel so … so great! I really needed that! I feel wonderful, almost like a miracle just happened!"

"Tell me more, Vivian."

"Well, I was walking down the street, feeling pretty low. I was thinking to myself, 'I wish I could go to confession. I really need to. It's been too, too long. And Easter is almost here. But it's so hard to find an opportunity for confession in this country!' "

Vivian is originally from Ecuador, we discover. Maybe she's feeling a little homesick here during Holy Week. She continues her story:

"Then, suddenly, this cheerful young person jumps in my path. 'Are you Catholic, miss?' 'Well, yes.' She gives me a rosary. And then she asks me, 'Have you been to confession lately? Our missionary priests are hearing confessions here.' I say, 'Are you kidding me? This is too weird! I was just walking along the street thinking I really needed to go to confession! How did you know that?' She says, 'I didn't. I just took a shot. Or maybe *He* just took a shot.' Then she walked me in. We were several blocks from the church, and she didn't want me to get lost. Can you believe that? What a kid! Do you know where I can find her?"

"Do you know how to get back to where you met her, Vivian?"

"Of course. I live near that corner."

"She'll be there."

Later in the evening, the missionary herself meets us. It's Deidre.

"I can't believe it! Vivian came all the way back to our corner to hug me! I feel like the whole mission was worth it for that one moment!

∞

Prince and Mott, SoHo
—Holy Thursday 2018

Long night tonight. Incredible day. Bob has just left to take in the confession signs from the approaching rain. The missionaries are already seated in the church. The priests are leaving the confessionals to vest for the one Mass they can give on Holy Thursday, the Mass of the Lord's Supper.

Outside, a single missionary stands alone in the fading light. The missionary of Wall Street.

He knows he's out of time. But for some reason he can't explain, he can't leave the corner. He's waiting for someone. He is not sure who, but someone is out there. One last soul.

Soon a middle-aged woman arrives. He approaches her.

"Excuse me, miss, are you Catholic?"

"Well, yes, I am. Is this St. Patrick's Old Cathedral?"

"That it is! Would you like to come into the church?"

"Yes, yes. Actually, I'm looking for someone named Evelyn. Do you know her?"

"I do. She's in the back of the church." That's where Evelyn —my wife—always is for these missions. She's the missionary at the back of the church who gently guides people in to confession when they've been sent in by the street missionaries.

"I met her Tuesday at the hospital," the woman says, "I need to find her."

Tears well up in my eyes. I know who this is. It's Maryann.

On Monday, Evelyn went into the hospital with a health emergency. We suspect it's related to her "treatable but incurable" blood cancer. After hundreds of prayers, many from people we had met that night on the streets of SoHo, she was released on Tuesday afternoon, the health crisis passed for the time being.

But while she was there, one of the nurses, not assigned to her, stopped by to visit. "I just wanted to come and say hello. I saw the rosary on your arm. Are you Catholic?"

"Yes, actually, I'm a Catholic missionary. The reason I was begging these doctors to let me go is that I'm on my way to the mission in SoHo."

"What mission?"

A long discussion. Maryann is struggling with a big issue.

She needs a priest. Tears are flowing on both sides. "Maryann," says Evelyn, "You need to come to SoHo. There's healing going on down there. The priest can help you."

"But I'm working all week!"

"Find a way. Maybe you can get someone to take a shift."

That was Tuesday. Now, two days later, Maryann has found a way. She's made it to SoHo, a minute before closing time.

"Maryann," I tell her, "I need to confess something to you. I know your story. I'm Evelyn's husband. She told me everything."

"Oh, my goodness! And you're here, waiting for me."

"I guess that's what the Lord wanted, Maryann. Let's go. It's almost closing time. All the priests need to leave the confessionals in a few minutes. On Holy Thursday, this is the only Mass they can give, so it's all hands on deck. But I promise you, Evelyn will get you a priest one way or another."

We rush into the church. Evelyn finds Fr. Donal and delivers Maryann, the last soul of the night. Maryann is reconciled and joins us for Mass.

In his homily, Msgr. Sakano reminds us of the transformative power of grace, of the upper room, and of how, by touching our hearts, Jesus gives us His. Jesus converts us into missionaries of His love. He takes us to the Promised Land.

Later, after Mass, Maryann, who has sat with us all evening, asks if she can come to Adoration in the crypt.

"Of course you can! All are welcome here. God loves you with all His heart, as much as He loves me or Evelyn."

"I do feel that, Steve. I feel I'm in the Promised Land."

∞

New York City
—April 5, 2018

Markets long since closed, office empty. Portfolios in good shape. I'm still here, putting the finishing touches on *The Missionary of Wall Street*. April 5 is my long-ago set deadline for sending this to the editors.

As evening falls, I get a call from Evelyn. She's fresh back from a follow-up visit to the hospital, where she had been sent for tests on the Monday of Holy Week.

"Steve, the good news is that my blood cancer hasn't gotten worse. My numbers are low but stable."

"Terrific, sweetheart! That's what we were praying for! What's the bad news?"

"They found a brain tumor."

We talk some more—about our plans, about our faith, about the mission, and how this latest turn of events would affect all of them.

"I'm optimistic, Steve! They found it early. I'm in the Lord's hands. And this really has me thinking about Maryann. If none of this had happened, I would never have met her in the hospital that night. Maybe this was for her."

Afterword

By
Msgr. Donald Sakano, Pastor
Basilica of St. Patrick's Old Cathedral

A priest's life is filled with an awareness of God's presence. Of course, people from every walk of life share in this sense of mystery, but a priest, as a shepherd of souls, enjoys a special vantage point, whereby, at the end of each day, he has an abundance of stories attesting to the certainty that the hand of God has been at work in his world. Sometimes the stories are boisterous and vivid, as when recalling a wedding, a baptism, or a vibrant session with the family religious-education program. And then there are the moments of a priest's day when God inserts Himself into events in a manner so unassuming we may have missed it. It's like when you have to watch an instant replay in order to catch what just happened. Those stories are sometimes the best, because they show how God can take you by surprise, a reminder that He is always active even when you don't call upon Him or expect His presence in something you consider mundane or unimportant.

My association with this mission of Christ in the streets of New York began more than ten years ago, when I asked the laypeople of Regnum Christi to help me re-evangelize my parish. Few of us could imagine the graces that followed. The missionaries started simply, endeavoring to do what the original disciples of Christ did: going out to the highways and the byways of a neighborhood, giving witness to the Good News of God's boundless mercy.

And as with all undertakings we do for the Lord with a spirit of love and adventure, the blessings bestowed on all—missioned and missionaries alike—have been boundless. Steve Auth, their leader from Wall Street, sensing something very special happening here, began capturing their stories each night as we gathered over dinner at our parish office on Mulberry, or more often, at Café Societal or "Louie's," next door to the church. This beautiful book is just one of the fruits of these efforts. It tells of not just his journey but the journey of all the missionaries.

During the days of mission on the streets surrounding my parish, the Basilica of St. Patrick's Old Cathedral, I am reminded of the underlying reason why the lay missionaries come back year after year. It is to experience what priests reflect on at the end of each day: the amazing power of God's long arms of mercy.

There is nothing like it. It is to participate in the same gift that prompted St. Paul to turn his life around and embark on his missionary journeys. It is to feel the same zeal that underscores the lives of the Christian martyrs. Once you have meted out the heavenly food of the gospel to people on the streets of a hungry neighborhood, I guarantee you will be back to do it again.

And again.

And again.

The best part about it all is that it takes no special ordination or education to be a missionary. God takes over. All you have to do is spread your spiritual wings a bit, and before you know it, you will be flying high. He will take you to delightful places.

Become a missionary!

Enjoy the ride!

—October 2018

Acknowledgments

Over the course of a decade, the stories in *The Missionary of Wall Street* were preserved in my notes from this very special street mission. Many of them are ones I was directly involved with, where I normally reference myself in the text as "a missionary," "our missionary," or "the missionary." Many others came to me from my fellow missionaries. Early on, I developed the habit of collecting each night the stories of the missionaries, listening intently as they excitedly told me of their adventures, keeping notes on my smartphone. Early the next morning, before the markets opened, I would synthesize these notes into a blog post, which I used both to thank the missionaries of the previous night and to inspire those who might be coming soon.

Sometimes, my fellow missionaries Bob Infanger and Evelyn Auth would write the posts for me. Collectively, these notes and posts form the stories used in this book. So, although I am listed as the author of this book, it really has many authors — the missionaries, the missioned, the brothers, and especially Bob and Evelyn. Without them, neither the mission nor this book would have come to pass.

THE MISSIONARY OF WALL STREET

More than a thousand missionaries, along with countless priests, brothers, sisters and consecrated women, and seminarians, have participated in the mission at Old St. Pat's since that first disjointed mission in 2009. Many are members of the Regnum Christi movement referenced in the text, though members of other religious orders, including the Franciscan Friars of the Renewal, the Sisters of Life, the Frassati Fellowship of NYC, and Opus Dei, along with diocesan priests, and just normal Church laity, have helped us over the years. I cannot name all the thousand-plus missionaries here, but a few stand out. B.J. and Jeannine Agugliaro joined almost from the start; they helped design the neighborhood coverage plan and stations described in chapter 3 and have led the important youth portion of the mission for many years. Ken and Cathy Sapeta, who showed up several years ago after having read a blog post, have been with us ever since in every season of the year, joyfully greeting passersby in front of the cupcake shop on Prince and Mott. Marie and John Hack, patient and confident, have never missed a mission and are always ready to take on any and all tasks. Bob's loving wife, Jody Infanger, has been the anchor of the church prayer team from its inception. The Regnum Christi New Jersey shore team, led by Dr. Julie Pineda and Dr. Pacita Sy, have traveled through good weather and bad to join us during some of the busiest seasons of the year. Angeli Kolhatkar developed the idea of the Adoration station and has managed that team from its inception. Other Regnum Christi stalwarts from the Tri-State area include Gabby and George Daus, Maria and Charly Spinelli, Sue Stone, and Lisa Rooney. Doug Dewey, active in the Opus Dei movement and in the Catholic business community in New York, fell in love with the mission a few years ago and has extended it uptown to St. Patrick's (New) Cathedral.

Acknowledgments

Many of my brothers from the Lumen Institute have participated in the mission over the years; two stalwarts who are always there when called are Ray Burns and Frank Randazzo. Glory Darbellay, a Consecrated Woman of Regnum Christi now, with national responsibilities in Washington, D.C., was a key organizational resource early on, when the rest of us were still trying to get our spiritual bearings. Although she has been away from the mission for many years, her spirit and energy remain. There are almost too many support staff to mention: the three dedicated parish maintenance men, Anthony Lewis, Eddie Rowe, and Jon Grodski, who've delivered enough sandwiches and pizzas to mission headquarters to feed a small army; the parish operations director, Chris Flatz, who is "all in" on the mission; and Rosa Jimenez, the parish admin executive, who has folded enough mission promotional pamphlets over ten years to fill a small FedEx truck. Ralph Didonato has shuttled the youth team around New York on his own bus at his own expense, year after year. On my end is the unflappable Mary Soressi, my loyal assistant who keeps the trains running on time, the prayer-card drawer stacked, the mission neighborhood maps fully stocked, and the mission blogs organized neatly.

Then there are the priests. Fr. John Bender, LC, based in the Cheshire seminary for the Legionaries of Christ, has happily endured many a long bus ride from Connecticut to bring his joyful seminarians to us on key nights in Holy Week and Advent. Two special diocesan priests who have helped us are Fr. Christopher Barkausen and Bishop John O'Hara. The priests from the Legionaries of Christ have been stalwart supporters and have been with us for every mission since the beginning. Three that seem born for the confessionals are Fr. Shawn Aaron, Fr. Jason Smith, and Fr. Michael Sliney. And then there is Msgr. Donald Sakano, who, over the course of the last decade, has become both a spiritual guide and a good friend. His loving support and enthusiasm have kept all of us going through many a long night. In many ways, all these holy priests have been the lead protagonists of this story; without them, none of this would have happened. Masters of the confessional, they lovingly and mercifully received, over the last decade, the thousands of lost souls we brought in from the streets. Many of these souls had not been to confession in years or even decades, yet our gentle priests always treated them with great love, dignity, and mercy. Although I could never get a peep out of them regarding their conversations, I frequently received this proclamation at the end of a long night: "Lots of big fish tonight, Steve! Really *big* fish!"

I also need to thank the wonderful editors of Sophia Institute Press and particularly Chris Bailey. Given that this was my first non-scholarly publication, the original manuscript had more than its fair share of loose ends, distractions, and literary cul-de-sacs. Their patience and creativity in editing the text while staying true to the mission's story was remarkable.

Finally, I want to thank the people of New York, who, despite their reputation for rudeness and toughness, are some of the most loving, and deeply spiritual people I've met. Their willingness to spend fifteen minutes on a street corner in SoHo going deep into matters of faith is quite remarkable. Although I've changed most of their names, their poignant stories of spiritual struggle and renewal speak to the depth of their character and the strength of their spirit. This book is their story as much as mine.

—Steve Auth
February 12, 2019

About the Author

Stephen Auth has had a long career on Wall Street, first with Prudential Investments in the 1980s and 1990s, and since 2000 with Federated Investors, where he serves as executive vice president and a chief investment officer of Federated Global Equities. Steve is a frequent guest on CNBC, Fox Business News, and Bloomberg TV, a long-standing participant in Barron's annual investment outlook panel, a member of The Economic Club of New York and The New York Society of Security Analysts, and a chartered financial analyst (CFA). He earned his undergraduate degree at Princeton University, where he graduated summa cum laude, and his graduate degree at Harvard Business School, where he was a Baker Scholar.

Steve is a member of the Regnum Christi movement and sits on the national board of the Lumen Institute, which he helped found in New York. He has participated in missions in Mexico, and with his wife, Evelyn, has led the New York City street mission for ten years. Steve and Evelyn are involved in a number of other apostolic activities, including a spiritual tour of the Metropolitan Museum of Art called "Man's Search for God: A History of Art through the Prism of Faith," which they developed and give on occasional Friday evenings. Steve also serves on the board of the Program for Church Management, being developed in Rome by the Pontifical University of the Holy Cross.

Steve and Evelyn have two wonderful sons, Richard and Michael Auth.

Sophia Institute

Sophia Institute is a nonprofit institution that seeks to nurture the spiritual, moral, and cultural life of souls and to spread the Gospel of Christ in conformity with the authentic teachings of the Roman Catholic Church.

Sophia Institute Press fulfills this mission by offering translations, reprints, and new publications that afford readers a rich source of the enduring wisdom of mankind.

Sophia Institute also operates two popular online Catholic resources: CrisisMagazine.com and CatholicExchange.com.

Crisis Magazine provides insightful cultural analysis that arms readers with the arguments necessary for navigating the ideological and theological minefields of the day. *Catholic Exchange* provides world news from a Catholic perspective as well as daily devotionals and articles that will help you to grow in holiness and live a life consistent with the teachings of the Church.

In 2013, Sophia Institute launched Sophia Institute for Teachers to renew and rebuild Catholic culture through service to Catholic education. With the goal of nurturing the spiritual, moral, and cultural life of souls, and an abiding respect for the role and work of teachers, we strive to provide materials and programs that are at once enlightening to the mind and ennobling to the heart; faithful and complete, as well as useful and practical.

Sophia Institute gratefully recognizes the Solidarity Association for preserving and encouraging the growth of our apostolate over the course of many years. Without their generous and timely support, this book would not be in your hands.

www.SophiaInstitute.com
www.CatholicExchange.com
www.CrisisMagazine.com
www.SophiaInstituteforTeachers.org